THE LEADER
YOU WANT TO BE

THE LEADER YOU WANT TO BE

Five Essential Principles for Bringing Out Your Best Self— Every Day

AMY JEN SU

HARVARD BUSINESS REVIEW PRESS

BOSTON, MASSACHUSETTS

The web addresses referenced in this book were live and correct at the time of the book's publication but may be subject to change.

Library of Congress Cataloging-in-Publication Data

Names: Su, Amy Jen, author.
Title: The leader you want to be : five essential principles for bringing
    out your best self—every day / Amy Jen Su.
Description: Boston, Massachusetts : Harvard Business Review Press, [2019] |
    Includes index. |
Identifiers: LCCN 2019024147 (print) | LCCN 2019024148 (ebook) |
    ISBN 9781633695917 (hardcover) | ISBN 9781633695917 (epub)
Subjects: LCSH: Leadership. | Executive ability. | Philosophy, Asian.
Classification: LCC HD57.7 .S8 2019 (print) | LCC HD57.7 (ebook) |
    DDC 658.4/092—dc23
LC record available at https://lccn.loc.gov/2019024147
LC ebook record available at https://lccn.loc.gov/2019024148

ISBN: 978-1-63369-591-7
eISBN: 978-1-63369-592-4

The paper used in this publication meets the requirements of the American National Standard for Permanence of Paper for Publications and Documents in Libraries and Archives Z39.48-1992.

To my son, Jordan, and husband, Greg—our family reminds me of what it means to have life purpose and the motivation to be my best self every day. Thank you for the love, support, and joy you bring.

CONTENTS

INTRODUCTION

A Tale of Two Leaders   1

Which Will You Be?

CHAPTER ONE

What Gets in the Way   17

The Pitfalls of Doing

CHAPTER TWO

The Power of Purpose   33

Reset Your Compass

CHAPTER THREE

The Power of Process   59

Reboot Your Personal Operating System

CHAPTER FOUR

The Power of People   93

Raise Your Game, Raise the Game of Others

CHAPTER FIVE

The Power of Presence   125

Don't Scratch the Itch

CHAPTER SIX

The Power of Peace   157

Loosen Your Grip

CHAPTER SEVEN

Pay It Forward   189

Create Leader A Teams and Organizations

APPENDIX

The Leader A Toolkit   207

The Leader A Master Checklist Tool   208

The Leader A Assessment   216

The Leader A Onboarding Worksheet Tool   217

Managing Overwork or Stress Worksheet Tool   219

Increasing Effectiveness, Discipline, Collaboration,
   or Satisfaction Tool   221

NOTES 223
INDEX 231
ACKNOWLEDGMENTS 239
ABOUT THE AUTHOR 243

THE LEADER
YOU WANT TO BE

A Tale of Two Leaders

Which Will You Be?

L eader A is the CEO of a thriving company. He has a big, ambitious vision and feels motivated to make a difference in his
industry. Having just secured additional funding, he's excited
by the growth potential of his organization. Today, Leader A has
just come out of a meeting with a candidate for one of the most
important positions he needs to fill on his leadership team. He's
totally fired up from telling the story of the organization and sharing his vision for where the business will be in five years. After
months of screening candidates, he feels like he might have finally
found the right person. He gets home still feeling energized and
enthusiastic. He's fully present at dinner with his family, and then
after the kids are in bed, he gets back online for a productive hour
that gives him a jump on the next day.

Leader B is also the CEO of a thriving company. He too has
vision, ambition, and the motivation to make a difference in his
industry. Today Leader B has just come out of a long day of back-
to-back meetings. Despite all the time he put in, he feels totally
frustrated by how little he accomplished. In one meeting he got lost
in the details, gave a knee-jerk reaction, and created an unnecessary fire drill for his team. At home, rather than listening to his wife

and kids during dinner, he feels irritated and distracted by the urge to get back on his computer. A couple of times he checks email on his cell phone, and immediately after dinner, he goes to his home office. After a few hours of work during which he feels like he's spinning his wheels, he collapses into bed, where he finds it difficult to fall asleep.

While it might be tempting to applaud Leader A and disapprove of Leader B, the reality is Leader A and Leader B are the same person.

Leader A and Leader B are representative of all of us. We've all had Leader A days when we felt especially effective, present, and satisfied with a job well done. When we're in Leader A mode, our energy and enthusiasm run high. We feel like we're making a difference, adding value, and having a positive impact. Our work feels meaningful, as if we're working not just to hit an external target but to fulfill a deep sense of purpose. Even if some days are jam-packed, they are, as one leader recently described it to me, "good-busy" days.

On the other hand, we're all familiar with Leader B mode. When Leader B has taken over, we may feel rushed, reactive, overwhelmed, or exhausted—or all of the above. We may feel like we're having little or no impact, or that no matter how much effort we expend, we're not moving the needle. Leader B days can be especially hard if you don't feel connected to other people or if you find yourself in conflict-heavy interactions. Another sign that we've slipped into Leader B mode is that we're more agitated, on edge, or irritable at home. All too often, it's our loved ones who are negatively affected when we take our work stress home.

The Rise and Costs of Leader B Mode

For the last two decades, I've been an executive coach working right alongside leaders and professionals in a wide variety of industries, roles, and stages of career. While my clients work for companies of different sizes and stages of growth, the one commonality among them all is that our coaching sessions are composed of some combination of celebrating Leader A successes and problem-solving for Leader B challenges. I know this dynamic well—like many of the folks I work with, I'm a full-time working parent as well as a leader of a growing firm. I'm walking the same tightrope, wanting to make a difference and achieve big goals while managing the inevitable stress and accountabilities of today's leadership demands.

While leadership will always involve some combination of Leader A and Leader B, over the past twenty years I've observed an escalation of conditions that increase the likelihood of Leader B mode. We're living in a time of rapid change, when a frenetic pace and an overfull plate are the norm—and sometimes even the ideal. Explicitly or implicitly, we're encouraged to work harder and faster and to put in more hours—all while technology and industry disruption are evolving more quickly than ever. It's no wonder that much of how business is conducted today has created a rising trend of Leader B days. Here are some of the most common challenges I hear:

- "Work is now 24-7. I'm never 'off,' even on the rare occasions I take personal time."

- "Since my promotion, I'm accountable for so much more. My boss says I need to rethink how I spend my time and energy and make sure I'm not in the weeds. I'm not even sure where to begin."

- "There's no time to do the things that matter, like develop my own skills or mentor others."

- "Everything is becoming so much more complex so quickly that I'm worried I can't keep up."

- "Imagining the future has become a luxury my division can't afford. We're all just trying to stay on top of the daily grind."

- "How do I maintain my own levels of motivation, much less my team's? I'm so tired."

With challenges like these, today's leaders risk falling into periods of disillusionment, ineffectiveness, dissatisfaction, and frustration. The cost of being stuck in Leader B mode is quite high; if left unchecked, it can even be career-ending. Here are some of the costs I've observed:

- CAREER DISSATISFACTION AND BURNOUT: Research shows that one in five highly engaged employees risks burnout, and that rather than experiencing greater satisfaction or joy, those most in demand often end up with the lowest engagement and career satisfaction over time.[1] A Deloitte survey of one thousand full-time employees in the United States found similar results: 77 percent had experienced burnout, even though 87 percent of respondents reported having "'passion for their job.'" In fact, among this latter group of highly engaged workers, 64 percent said they were frequently stressed. At the same time, nearly seven in ten people (69 percent) said they felt their employer "does not do enough to minimize burnout," while one in five (21 percent) said they don't believe their employer offers any stress-reduction programs.[2] All of this adds up to a lot of Leader B days, and many of us wonder if the day-to-day sacrifices are even worth it.

- STALLED CAREERS AND THE INABILITY TO SCALE: Most of us want to get promoted, take on more significant roles, and achieve more. However, I've seen folks stuck in Leader B mode who stall out as their organizations grow, and they can't keep pace. My colleague and good friend Betty Hung, an operating principal of Vista Equity Partners and one of the most senior women in the private-equity industry, once summed up this reality so well: "When you get promoted to bigger roles with new and greater responsibilities, you have to reinvent yourself (over and over) and accelerate your velocity, pace, and effectiveness. The curve gets exponentially steeper in terms of complexity and expectations—it's not linear. But how can you keep improving and growing at that rate? To be successful, you need to take more than just incremental steps. But there's not really a human equivalent of Moore's Law. . . ."[3]

- NEGATIVE IMPACT ON HEALTH: One of the biggest personal consequences of being stuck in Leader B mode is the toll it can take on our health. I've experienced this myself at points in my career when I've gained weight, suffered from chronic back and neck pain, and struggled with bouts of bronchitis and asthma from overwork and stress. Clients have shared similar struggles with insomnia, migraines, and other health issues. A recent study suggested that work-related stress over a one-year period in the United Kingdom accounted for 37 percent of all ill-health cases and 45 percent of all working days lost due to illness across all industries and professions. Workload pressure (including tight deadlines and too much responsibility) and lack of managerial support were the main factors employees cited as causing work-related stress.[4] In the United States, the psychological and physical consequences of burnout come with health-care costs ranging from $125 billion to $190 billion a year—which is to say nothing of the cost that low productivity across organizations, high turnover, and the loss of talent brings.[5]

- NEGATIVE RIPPLE EFFECT ON TEAMS, ORGANIZATIONS, AND LOVED ONES: The costs of Leader B mode don't stop with us. Like a set of dominoes, your Leader B "ripple effect" cascades out, potentially creating more Leader B days for others. Not only are you not operating at your best, but team spirit, performance, and collaboration can suffer as you telegraph stress or impatience onto teammates and loved ones. Ron Carucci, the author of *Rising to Power*, poignantly captures this all-too-common dynamic: "Confronted with intense levels of stress amidst turbulent change or the headwinds of a harsh market, leaders' fuses get short. . . . Administrative assistants, unwitting family members, or direct reports trying to help can often bear the brunt of misplaced frustrations."[6]

The Benefits and Rewards of Leader A Mode

If you're thinking this all sounds pretty grim, you're right. But the good news vastly outweighs the bad: no matter how long you've been in Leader B mode, there is *always* a way back to living and leading from your highest and best self. Even a taste of Leader A mode is enough to keep many of us in the game because the experience is so rewarding. When we're consistently in Leader A mode, we have a sense of our purpose and impact, we're especially effective, and we experience the growth that comes from learning and challenge. Like the dedicated golfer who gets frustrated with the inevitable bad shots along the course, we keep playing for those moments when our swing is perfect and we hear that singular "ping" as the ball sails across the green toward the flag. We can even see that all those frustrating shots were just part of the game—no effort is wasted.

Here's a glimpse of the benefits of being in Leader A mode:

- IMPACT: There's nothing like feeling as if you've added value, uniquely contributed to your team or organization, or demonstrated your expertise. In Leader A mode, we know our skills and knowledge make a difference.

- RESULTS: There is great satisfaction in meeting our goals, achieving key milestones, or delivering superior results.

- MEANING: Our careers provide tremendous opportunity to engage in meaningful work, enjoy what we do, and feel a sense of achievement. They also provide tremendous opportunity to pay it forward by mentoring someone at an earlier stage of career.

- CONNECTION: Some of life's deepest connections come from being part of a team working toward a common goal. If you haven't yet experienced this at work, maybe you have through sports, military service, or involvement with a civic or charitable group. Whatever the context, the feeling of being "in flow" with your colleagues is compelling enough to keep many people in Leader A mode.

- CREATIVITY: Work can provide a context in which we can create something of value that is altogether new. In philosophy, this concept is called *Poiesis*. Derived from the ancient Greek verb that means "to make," poiesis is "the activity in which a person brings something into being that did not exist before."[7] Whether it's a product, a service, an idea, or a process, bringing new things to the marketplace is tremendously exciting and keeps our passion ignited.

- GROWTH: Many people I know could have chosen to stay in the same roles they were in five years ago, in jobs where they were fully skilled and perhaps had more free time. But remaining in familiar roles can mean ignoring our drive, ambition, and intellectual curiosity and missing out on the innovation, progress, and expansion that's part of the Leader A experience. As one leader recently shared with me, he made a job change into a much more intense, fast-paced organization because the new role not only preserved his love for the industry but also offered an exciting, steep learning curve he thrived on.

The Doorway to Leader A: Using the Five Ps

Given the climate of business today—marked by velocity and ferocity—how do we create and sustain the conditions that support Leader A mode, and when we do slip into Leader B mode, how do we get back on track, quickly and with self-compassion?

What I've found after working with thousands of ambitious and successful leaders, as well as learning from my own professional experience, is that today's leadership challenges call for a new approach. When volatility, uncertainty, complexity, and ambiguity—VUCA, as the military call it—characterize the context in which we're called upon to lead, we can no longer get by with quick fixes like sharpening our time-management skills or looking for life hacks that increase productivity. Instead, we need a whole-person approach that's grounded in a continuous level of self-awareness and self-care.

What do I mean by a whole-person approach? At the simplest level, I'm referring to an approach that addresses a leader's external and internal worlds. Ultimately, effective leadership must attend not only to a leader's external world of effectiveness—things like results, progress, and output—but also to the leader's internal world—drivers, motivations, and influences. Any leadership approach that will sustain you over the course of a career as you continue to grow and take on bigger roles requires a deep, honest look inward as well as an outward gaze to remain mindful of your impact.

Over my twenty years of working with leaders, I've identified five essential principles that are common to effective leadership in any context, and that are built upon this whole-person approach. They are the key areas that support Leader A mode, get us back on track when Leader B mode takes over, and help us take on increasingly larger roles or opportunities while sustaining our highest and best selves. With the busy leader in mind, I've made these principles concrete, practical, and easy to use, and I've organized them in a simple yet holistic framework called the *five Ps*. We'll explore each one in depth in later chapters, but here's a brief summary:

The Five Ps

1. PURPOSE: Remain grounded in your passions and contributions. It takes conviction to ensure you are doing your highest and best work and that your work has meaning and is making a difference.

2. PROCESS: Rely on daily practices and routines that honor your natural energy rhythms, enhance performance, save time, help you restore, and provide critical guardrails that keep you on point.

3. PEOPLE: Raise your game by raising the game of others at work and at home. Increase your resilience with healthier boundaries and rules of engagement with others.

4. PRESENCE: Strengthen your inner capacity to pause between stimulus and response, so matters of effectiveness and impact drive decisions and actions, rather than old habits or knee-jerk impulses.

5. PEACE: Learn to trust your capacities to evolve, adapt, and respond to whatever comes your way. Lead from a place of acceptance, gratitude, and trust, rather than a place of stress, striving, and ego protection.

When I use the five Ps, the following image always comes to mind. Purpose sits at the top, as how we define our highest and best guides all our actions. Along the left I picture the next two Ps, people and process, as levers that connect to a leader's external world. They're critical to effectiveness and to expanding external capacity, bandwidth, and scale. Along the right side are presence and peace, levers that connect to a leader's internal world. They're

FIGURE I-1

The five P framework

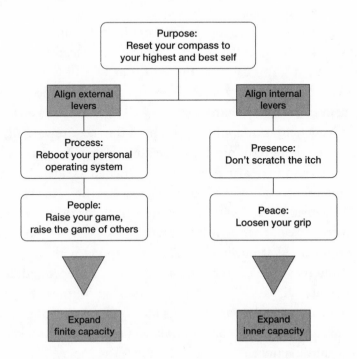

critical to emotional resilience and satisfaction, and to expanding our inner ability to loosen the grip and trust in who we are and what we've accomplished.

Think of each P as a doorway—an entry point to your highest and best self. You can access and examine any of the five Ps at any time. You can align and realign with them as many times a day as you need to. Accessing any of the five Ps will give you a sense of agency and control when things start to feel out of control, because the very moment you hit the pause button and attend to any of the five Ps, you're already shifting to Leader A mode. And because they work in concert, attending to one P will automatically enrich and align the other four.

I've witnessed those who've used the five Ps over the long term grow into ever more challenging roles and become sought-after leaders and influential mentors in their fields, while at the same time being more centered, calm, and fulfilled than they've ever been. You know these leaders when you encounter them: they're at the top of their game, leading major organizations or maybe even entire industries, and doing so while remaining centered and inspiring others to do and be their own personal best. Such an outcome is perhaps the pinnacle of leadership.

These leaders bring to mind a concept from the ancient Chinese belief system Taoism called *wu-wei*, which can be translated as "actionless action." You can also think of it as effortless action, or if you prefer, being "in the zone." Wu-wei is about living in a state of alignment or harmony, with others as well as within ourselves, and from a leadership standpoint, it is one of the most rewarding outcomes of the long-term practice of leading from a Leader A mindset. As its paradoxical nature suggests, when Leader A is your operating norm, your efforts become more effortless, the value you provide is invaluable, and though you're probably busier than ever, you enjoy a greater sense of fulfillment and ease. When something does go amiss, as it inevitably will, you respond with more equanimity and poise. You realize and accept that Leader A and Leader B modes are all part of the whole leadership journey. You don't panic when you find yourself in Leader B mode because, as with any long road with peaks and valleys, you trust you're still heading in the right direction.

What's in This Book—and How to Use It

My first book, *Own the Room: Discover Your Signature Voice to Master Your Leadership Presence*, written with my colleague and good friend Muriel Maignan Wilkins, was about helping leaders build their leadership presence by making a more authentic connection to others. *The Leader You Want to Be* looks at how to tap into and expand a powerful inner *and* outer capacity for leadership by making a more authentic connection to yourself.

This book is built on three foundational tenets: *self-care*, *self-awareness*, and *personal agency*. Taking care of yourself is a prerequisite for the Leader A experience. One CEO I worked with put it beautifully: "Self-care is hardly some selfish thing," he said. "Care of oneself should be part of the mandate for every job." I couldn't agree more. Effective leadership requires an understanding of the conditions that cultivate our highest and best contributions and our deepest and most inspiring passions. In short, proper self-care enables us to do and be our best. It's not something we can squeeze in at the end of a long day or put off until we can get around to it. On the contrary, it's an urgent *daily* responsibility whose importance can no longer be overlooked or underestimated. Throughout the book, I'll show you some new ways to integrate self-care into the workday and into your routine.

Self-awareness is just as necessary. So many of us are so busy that we barely stop to check in with ourselves or look at a situation from a more objective, thoughtful viewpoint. But using the five Ps requires you to use what many call the "inner spectator," which is the part of yourself that can see your behavior, thoughts, and actions from a calm, objective point of view, even in the midst of the busiest of schedules. In varying contexts this inner spectator has also been called the observer self, the impartial observer, the ever-present self, the inner witness, and, one of my favorites, "the one inside who is not busy."[8] Yes, even the busiest of us has a "spectating self" that resides within, a self that is protected from the fray and is always calm, always centered. I'm most drawn to the way LinkedIn CEO Jeff Weiner, who has a 97 percent employee approval rating and is widely regarded as one of the most beloved CEOs in the world, describes it.[9] In an interview with Oprah Winfrey on her *SuperSoul Sunday* show, Weiner explained that the ability to be a "spectator to your own thoughts, especially when you become emotional," is one of the most important lessons he's learned and one of the keys to happiness.[10] I'm particularly drawn to his use of "spectator" because it conjures the image of periodically coming off the playing field where the drama of the day-to-day game is happening so we can see ourselves in action, even as the action is unfolding.

The inner spectator will function as our tour guide through the five Ps, and throughout the book we'll be learning how to flex the muscle of self-spectating. The fact is, most leaders already have within them what they need to lead like Leader A. The five Ps provide a way to tap into what's already there—and to remind us to look within, which can be easy to forget when we're exhausted, overwhelmed, or already on the slippery slope to burnout. I'll show you how to access your inner spectator and then how to cultivate it, building and strengthening it like a muscle, so you can come to rely on it to support and sustain Leader A.

And finally, there's personal agency, or the power we have to make a choice. When we're in Leader B mode, it may feel like we've run out of options. But with a Leader A lens, we can see avenues and options that were there all along but simply hidden when we're overextended, when we're not getting the self-care we need, or when one of the Ps needs a tune-up. Over time, habitually attending to the five Ps enables us to live into the truth that we *always* have a choice in how we show up every day—in every meeting, through every email, and at every moment. The five Ps help us see our personal agency and increase the chances that we spend more of our time in Leader A mode.

While the advice you'll read here is culled from my years of working with leaders as an executive coach, strategic planner, and management consultant, you'll also find ideas and tools drawn from my background and certifications in yoga, my experience with meditation, and my personal experience as a first-generation child of Asian immigrants. Though I was born and raised in the United

States, from my earliest memory a thread of Eastern culture and philosophy has run through my life, and I'm pleased to see the growing interest in Eastern practices in the broader world, in everything from health and wellness to management and leadership.

So you may see a concept presented through the lens of a university professor's research or, as you've seen already, through the words of Lao Tzu, the father of Taoism—sometimes even in the same paragraph! Whatever their source, all the tools I present are meant to be tactical, no-nonsense, and ready-to-implement. And, where it's applicable, I draw on the lessons I am still learning as a leader trying to make a difference and hold it all together each day. I'm the first to admit I don't have it all figured out; this book is as much the result of my own daily struggle to manage the tensions of contemporary leadership as it is my mission to help others lead with more consciousness, ability, and ease. But here you'll find the best of what I've learned about how to create your own personal playbook for being Leader A, and you'll find many real-life stories of leaders who've used the five Ps to get an accurate read on their situations and then quickly align to the vision and goals they have for their organizations, their teams, and themselves.

You'll also find an abundance of frameworks, tools, tips, ideas, and exercises in every chapter. Thus, I'd recommend reading the book over multiple sittings, and over time experimenting to see what supports your personal best and Leader A. You may not even want to read the five Ps in the order they're presented. If you know immediately, for instance, that your processes are keeping you in Leader B mode, start with chapter 3. Or if you're aware that you have a tendency to be hard on yourself and what you need is more inner peace, you can skip ahead to chapter 6. Wherever you begin, you can always return to the other Ps later. Though each P is explained separately, as we proceed you'll come to see how they all work together, influencing and informing each other.

Chapter 1 will begin by taking a closer look at the day-to-day realities and challenges of being an ambitious, successful leader in today's fast-paced, intense, and complex workplace. We will see how these challenges lead us into common coping mechanisms and predictable "pitfalls of doing" that increase our stress, ineffectiveness, and dissatisfaction. We'll also see how it's possible, by using a Leader A lens, to transform those very pitfalls into performance enhancers.

Chapter 2 introduces the first P, *purpose*, and discusses how getting anchored in your purpose at work can lift you out of Leader B mode. We'll look at how purpose evolves and manifests differently over time, and I'll give you a concrete, practical tool that will guide you in how to gain clarity on your highest and best use. Chapter 2 will also show you how getting grounded in your purpose creates a way to sift your yesses and nos to prioritize your workload and ensure you are leading with passion and contribution.

In chapters 3 and 4, we'll look at two Ps—*process* and *people*— that impact the leader's outer world of effectiveness, discipline, and sustainability. In chapter 3, we will look at how you can create processes that fit you and your context, protect your time, and restore your energy. In chapter 4, we'll take a look at the strength of your team and your strategic network of support, and we'll explore how to set healthy boundaries.

In chapters 5 and 6, we'll turn our attention to two Ps—*presence* and *peace*—that focus on the leader's inner world. In chapter 5, we'll discuss how you can be more present even when distraction, procrastination, or self-sabotage threaten to get the best of you. This chapter will also show you how to cultivate your self-awareness so your actions come less from a state of reaction and more from a place of thoughtful, considered reasoning. In chapter 6, you will learn more about how to let go so you're less focused on striving and protecting your ego and more able to access acceptance, contentment, and trust. The present and peaceful leader is able to operate from an inner place of calm, equanimity, and confidence, no matter the situation at hand.

With all the Ps in place, chapter 7 will discuss how you can pay it forward and use the five Ps to develop other Leader A leaders, teams, and organizations. While ambitious leaders will always be evolving and developing individually, the ultimate in leadership is mentoring others and helping our teams and organizations sustain, scale, and thrive.

Finally, the appendixes at the end of the book will provide you with tools that will help you see "where you're at" and get a quick read on the best response to whatever leadership challenge you're facing.

My hope is that you'll read this book as if we're in a coaching session together. Throughout the book I'll lay out for you the same concepts, leadership tools, and exercises my clients have successfully used to grow into the leaders they want to be. My aim is to honor your whole person while appreciating the unique organizational context and world within which you operate. I hope you'll feel free to experiment and see which tools work best for you and your particular leadership role.

Today's leadership challenges are formidable, but if you are attending to your highest and best self—the outer forces of your roles and responsibilities, as well as the inner drives and passions that fuel your desire to lead—challenges become opportunities. Leadership presents at every moment an unparalleled possibility to learn, innovate, grow, mentor, and make a significant difference in the world. It presents at every moment the opportunity to discover your highest and best self, to become more deeply aware of yourself as well as the world around you, to hold a broad, capacious perspective, and to fulfill a purpose the world needs that is wholly, uniquely yours to give.

CHAPTER ONE

What Gets in the Way
The Pitfalls of Doing

Whether you are a leader of an organization, team, family, community, or school group—or like most of us, some combination thereof—each day you are faced with many moments that test your ability to lead effectively. Decisions need to be made, work needs to be prioritized, and initiatives need to be coordinated with colleagues, all of whom have their own agendas, styles, and perspectives. The landscape of contemporary life is pocked with challenges for *all* professionals, irrespective of industry, level, or skill. Many of these challenges lead us down a slippery slope right into Leader B mode, where things start to look more difficult by the day.

We can all come up with our own lists, but I've found that these challenges fall into four general categories. See if any of these sound familiar:

1. THERE ARE NEVER ENOUGH HOURS IN THE DAY. This may be the number one challenge I hear, and it's one I struggle with most myself. Many of us face the constant quandary of wanting to do more, advance and complete our initiatives, expand our impact in new and exciting ways, and be the best

version of ourselves we can be. But we're all limited by the finite hours in any given day. Our challenge is figuring out how to get everything done within that set framework—and without sacrificing too much of the things that make life meaningful outside of work, such as time with family and friends, personal interests, and exercise.

2. WORK IS MORE COMPLEX. Many leaders are grappling with overwhelming complexity on multiple fronts. It seems that the problems we are being asked to solve are becoming more complex, and more and more of us are working in complicated matrixed environments where many hands need to touch an issue but often without clear accountability or decision-making rights. Meanwhile, work is becoming more global, which brings its own set of challenges: what to centralize and decentralize, how to work within and navigate different cultures, and how to work virtually with colleagues in multiple locations and time zones.

3. OUR ORGANIZATIONS AND OTHER PEOPLE GET IN THE WAY. Our bosses, peers, direct reports, and other stakeholders can create frustration, unnecessary roadblocks, bottlenecks, or conflict. Most organizational cultures today emphasize intensity and encourage long hours. The examples of roadblocks that come from external sources are endless. A toxic work environment, an underperforming team member, differing visions, poor planning, unclear or unreasonable expectations, a lack of support, budgetary restrictions, competing priorities, conflict with a colleague or boss . . . any of these can get in the way of our progress.

4. WE GET IN OUR OWN WAY. Highly ambitious, successful people tend to be more self-critical, place greater demands on themselves, and generally feel an outsized pressure to succeed. Many leaders bear the weight of performance pressure and accountability more heavily than others, while quietly we harbor self-doubt and a deep fear of failure. These are the issues that are borne from within—our inner drives, natural

inclinations, and motivating factors—and they're often deep-rooted, part of our psychological makeup. Professor and leadership researcher Laura Empson points out that high achievers tend to blame themselves when they feel inadequate, taking colleagues' success as confirmation of their own inadequacy. In an effort to conceal their perceived shortcomings, they don't share their struggles with their colleagues, "thus perpetuating the myth of the invincible professional, which encourages their colleagues to feel inadequate in turn."[1]

Which Lens—Leader A or B?

The truth is, we *all* struggle from time to time, and we all have days in which we regret how we responded to or handled something. Finite "clock" time will never go away, the work ahead will likely become more complex, difficulties and conflicts with other people are bound to crop up from time to time, and naturally, our organizations will continue to have their ups and downs. With these conditions in place, every professional I know—and certainly I include myself here—fluctuates between Leader A and Leader B mode. The image that comes to mind for me is of an internal teeter-totter—we all have our up days and down days, shifting back and forth from A to B and back again. I wish I could tell you that I've figured out how to be Leader A all day, every day, but what I've come to realize is that the very expectation to be Leader A 100 percent of the time is not only unrealistic, it's actually a surefire way to slip into Leader B mode.

The real danger is that if we are not aware, we can end up in Leader B mode for so long that it becomes our operating norm, and not only do we become less effective, but so do our teams and possibly our organizations. So how can we recognize when we start to shift from Leader A to Leader B? And how can we recognize the triggers that set us on the slippery slope?

The first step toward answering these is to recognize that the lens is variable. If we're looking out at the world through a Leader

A lens, problems look like opportunities for us to flex our expertise and hone our skills. We feel energized, fully present, and satisfied as a leader, even during those inevitable crunch times. We're like the surfer who doesn't fight the current but works with it, using it to her advantage to ride right into the perfect wave.

On the other hand, if we're looking at the world through a Leader B lens, we may find ourselves whipped off the board and struggling against the waves. When we're in a Leader B mindset, problems can feel insurmountable, and we may find that our effectiveness, presence, and internal satisfaction have been compromised.

Falling into the Four Pitfalls of Doing

What I have come to understand is that more often than not, the shift from the clear-eyed view of Leader A into Leader B's cloudy vision begins as a coping mechanism. In response to some sort of challenge or uncertainty, we turn to our go-to form of relief. This makes perfect sense, as all coping mechanisms offer a short-term benefit, such as temporary relief from anxiety and stress. But inevitably, most coping mechanisms reach their limits, and if relied on too long, they can lead us into a deeper hole. The progression can look like this.

I've found that there are four types of pitfalls we typically fall into, which keep us in a cycle of stress, ineffectiveness, negativity, or feeling overwhelmed. I call them the Four Pitfalls of Doing:

- The I'll Just Do More Pitfall

- The I'll Just Do It Now Pitfall

- The I'll Just Do It Myself Pitfall

- The I'll Just Do It Later Pitfall

FIGURE 1-1

A slippery slope

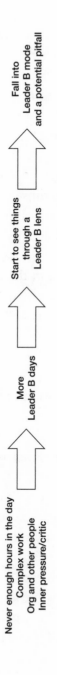

Never enough hours in the day
Complex work
Org and other people
Inner pressure/critic

More
Leader B days

Start to see things
through a
Leader B lens

Fall into
Leader B mode
and a potential pitfall

The following section describes each of the pitfalls in detail, and I recommend reading it twice. Sometimes it's easier to think about others before turning the focus on ourselves, so the first time through, think of a colleague, direct report, or someone you are mentoring and consider whether one of these pitfalls might be at play for them. Then, come back to the beginning of the section and read it again, thinking about how the pitfalls apply to you.

The I'll Just Do More Pitfall

There will always be more to do than we have the hours in the day to do it. Most tempting to those with a high bias to action, the I'll Just Do More Pitfall leads us into a false comfort zone crammed with volume, motion, and activity.

The mindset: When we're in the I'll Just Do More Pitfall, we believe that as long as we keep working—harder and longer—we'll be able to add more value, get ahead of others, get more out of life, or just feel okay.

In this mindset, our lens becomes clouded with all that's going on, and we lose vital track of how our work and choices are connected to passion, contributions, meaning, or progress. Instead, we get caught on a hamster wheel of *doing*, of sheer activity, and despite our strenuous efforts, we don't get the results we hope for and we don't have a sense of internal satisfaction in what we're getting done.

This mindset is easy to fall into because the world around us tells us this is what we should be doing to succeed. Greg McKeown, author of the book *Essentialism: The Disciplined Pursuit of Less*, describes the "more" bubble in which we somehow feel we must do it all, have it all, or achieve it all. More than any other time in history, McKeown explains, we are aware of what others are doing, which subsequently influences what we believe we "should" be doing. As a result, says McKeown, "We have been sold a bill of goods: that success means being supermen and superwomen who can get it all done. . . . Not only are we addicted to the drug of more, we are pushers too. In the race to get our children into 'a good college,' we have added absurd amounts of homework, sports, clubs, dance performances and ad infinitum extracurricular activities. And with them, busyness, sleep deprivation and stress."[2]

The mode: For a while we can derive the benefits of the I'll Just Do More Pitfall, but they are usually short-lived. It may feel good temporarily to be needed by others, demonstrate that you have a high tolerance for stress, or relish the excitement of taking on something new. But eventually you hit a point of diminishing returns.

You know you're in a full-on pitfall when you feel overwhelmed, like the weight of the world is on your shoulders. While you take pride in being someone others need or count on, in this pitfall you start to resent the people you've been trying to support, or you begin to resent those you see leaving the office earlier, or perhaps friends or loved ones who are in jobs or have life situations where they work fewer hours or don't work at all.

When you're in this pitfall, you feel exhausted and wonder when you can get off the hamster wheel. Each time a new request comes into your inbox, you experience it as an imposition rather than an opportunity. Despite your complaining and venting to friends and family, you find it increasingly harder to say no, and keep saying yes. You often hear the voice in your head insisting you "should" do it. And on projects, you often do more than is required just because you can.

The consequences: In addition to physical and mental exhaustion and eventual burnout, the toughest consequence I've seen from the I'll Just Do More Pitfall is career stall-out. This happens when the hardworking professional has done everything the organization has asked but then hits a ceiling in terms of the next promotion. Instead of applauding your long hours and hard work, your boss begins to question if you have the chops to do anything other than churn out high volumes of work. You've cemented your status as the "worker bee" and can't progress to the next level.

The I'll Just Do It Now Pitfall

If the first pitfall is about our relationship to volume, then the second is about our relationship to time.

Looming deadlines, long to-do lists, and overfull inboxes are all realities in modern work life. Meeting deadlines and getting stuff done quickly are important. However, when we've fallen into the I'll Just Do It Now pitfall, we've started to overdose on adrenaline, and our responses become knee-jerk and impulsive.

The mindset: The Leader B mindset in this pitfall becomes fixated on getting things done ASAP. You begin to cope by believing that as long as you use your speed and ability to push, then all will be well. The thrill of crossing things off the list does give some temporary relief—until you realize the list is endless.

The mode: Rather than demonstrating an appropriate level of urgency for the situation at hand, you've fallen into a constant state of emergency. Rushing is your operating norm. Your conversations, meetings, and emails are all marked by an intensity and sense of urgency that is disproportionate to what the situation calls for. People get blasted with one-liners from your cell phone without context or clarity. In meetings, you dive right in without setting much context or an agenda. In 360 reviews, others may describe you as reactive, abrupt, or overly focused on execution.

We all need to sprint from time to time, but the healthy dose of adrenaline that fuels a push now goes haywire—your body is nearly always tense and contracted, and you start to hold your breath or shallow-breathe as adrenaline and unhealthy levels of cortisol flood your veins. You hear every ding of your email or phone and react immediately, with a constant glance at technology or social media. Your nervous system feels like it's in overdrive, and the coffee and snacks you grab on the run only worsen your agitated state. You radiate tension and stress as you power through the day in a state of fight-or-flight reaction.

The consequences: When you stay in this mode too long, you might find that when you finally slow down, even a little bit, you end up getting sick because you've finally let your guard down. On the career front, you start to experience the downside of being overbiased toward (urgent) execution: you run the risk of getting pegged with a reputation as the "fix-it" person who just isn't strategic enough for more senior roles.

Your teams and organization may feel the brunt of this pitfall. Your internal voice screaming at you to "get it done *now*" telegraphs outward; even if you don't say so explicitly, others pick up on that pressure and start to think, "You better get this done ASAP!" Your team begins to experience each ask, whim, or reaction from you as gospel, putting everyone into a constant state of high alert.

The I'll Just Do It Myself Pitfall

There will always be things we are able to do better or faster than others, and there will always be things we want done a certain way. And frankly, there will always be things we simply love doing ourselves.

But there comes a point when our instinct to do everything ourselves creates an overdependence on us. When we refuse to wean ourselves off a task and insist on doing it all ourselves, we can create bottlenecks that are detrimental to ourselves, to our teams, and to the goals we're trying to achieve.

The mindset: This mindset is guided by the false belief that you must do everything by yourself or that you have to rescue others. Either can feel really good temporarily, for any number of reasons. Perhaps you do something yourself because it's fun even though it's no longer your highest and best use in a larger role. Or maybe you love the sweet taste of moving quickly and keeping control of something that you know you're able to do faster and better than others. Or perhaps you feel relief from avoiding the conflict of difficult performance discussions or tough personnel decisions by taking on things in order to protect an employee who's been loyal to you or has worked for you for a long time. Whatever the under-lying motivation, at some point you end up feeling overloaded, feeling more stressed, or doing more than your fair share.

The mode: When you've fallen into the I'll Just Do It Myself Pitfall, others keep coming directly to you, rather than your team, for infor-mation or deliverables. You get involved in many conversations and decisions, and often, your team feels they don't have the autonomy to deliver on their own—they have to wait to talk to you first. You often say things like, "Oh, I'll just handle it" or "He's going to get there—I just need to give him more time and don't mind taking on some of the pieces until then." Even when others offer to help, you ignore or re-fuse them. Your go-to response is, "No worries, I got this."

The consequences: By routinely doing things that others could do for you or by doing things yourself because you're compensating for a weak performer on your team, you can become a bottleneck and end up compromising your vision. Ultimately, if you remain in this pitfall, you won't be able to scale beyond your own capacity, and you risk inhibiting growth not only for yourself but for your team and your company. This often leads to incremental progress rather than the breakthroughs or transformations many companies are looking for.

The I'll Just Do It Later Pitfall

While the first three pitfalls are about coping by exerting your will or finding a way to feel like you're still in control when things around you feel uncertain or out of control, this fourth pitfall is about procrastination or putting yourself last.

The mindset: This mindset kicks in when we assume that we'll get to important things that matter to ourselves later. For example, your goal for getting in shape or taking more vacation this year can get shuffled down the priority list when other things seem more important—yet again. You find yourself making excuses like, "Something else came up," "I'm just too busy," or "I'll get to that eventually."

The mode: You find yourself often frustrated that you're putting off important things. Other people's needs—or indeed any other need that comes up—take priority over your own agenda, and you find yourself continually sidetracked. There could be an underlying conflict avoidance in play, or perhaps you have weak boundaries with others, either of which makes it easier to put yourself and your own priorities last. Or there could be an underlying fear of failure that's causing resistance to working toward your goals. Whatever the cause, it can feel like you're not performing up to your potential. You are relentless in reminding yourself of what you're not accomplishing, and you may struggle with a constant thrum of anxiety about not meeting your goals.

The consequences: The impact on ourselves can be hard in this pitfall. While others' needs are being met, your own health, well-being, networks, relationships, and professional or personal growth are compromised. You don't fully embrace an opportunity, or you miss one altogether. You risk not moving the ball forward on an important or meaningful project, and at work, your contribution can plateau. Putting off or ignoring the big initiatives and objectives, over time, has the potential to derail or even end a career, and the stress of remaining in this pitfall can easily lead to negative impacts on health and relationships.

As I mentioned at the start of this section, it's often easier to think about the pitfalls in the context of what's happening for other people rather than for ourselves. In my case, it's always been easier for me to spot a pitfall happening for a client than for myself. After all, holding up the mirror is never easy.

There was a point during the writing of this book, for example, when I realized I wasn't going to meet my publisher's deadline. This was a painful realization. I was disappointed in myself and embarrassed. I'd told all my colleagues and friends about the book schedule. And I couldn't figure out how I'd gotten to this place, after six months of intense work and a desk littered with edited drafts, notes, new pages, and Post-it notes. Even after all that time and effort, I didn't have a manuscript I was happy with, and I was increasingly overwhelmed and stressed.

When I took a step back to observe the situation, the irony nearly bowled me over: during the book-writing process, I'd experienced *every* Pitfall of Doing.

I had not fully appreciated the extra workload the book would add to my already full schedule. I assumed I could *just do more* and control and push my way to a manuscript. My anxiety mounted as the deadline loomed, and any time it peaked, I'd feel a surge of adrenaline and my mind would convince me I could *just do it now*. So there I sat, reactively and impulsively typing away, but not producing my highest-quality work. Then, because I had one book under my belt already, instead of asking for help I tried to *just do it myself*. But inevitably, client work would come to the forefront, and I'd procrastinate on the book and convince myself I could *just do it later*.

It was a sobering wake-up call to realize I had fallen into the pitfalls I'd been writing about. Ultimately, it was good to lift out of the noise and look at what was happening with a more clear-eyed view and get honest with myself. Following is the exercise I used to assess the situation. You can use it whenever you feel like you've slipped into Leader B mode.

EXERCISE
Assessing the Pitfalls of Doing

This exercise has the potential to raise some discomfort. Yet it's vitally important to pause regularly and do some honest self-spectating. This exercise can be especially helpful to get you back on track when a situation, project, or initiative isn't going the way you'd hoped.

1. Take several moments to reflect on a project, initiative, or goal that isn't going the way you'd hoped or planned. As much as you can, observe the situation *without judgment*.

2. Now identify which of the pitfalls might be at play and getting in the way.

3. Finally, use table 1-1 to assess what is happening.

TABLE 1-1

Assessing the pitfalls of doing

Pitfall	What does it look like or sound like for you at this time?	What emotions or feelings is it bringing up?	What is the impact on you, your goal, or others?	What is an action you can take to shift out of this pitfall?
I'll Just Do More				
I'll Just Do It Now				
I'll Just Do It Myself				
I'll Just Do It Later				

As you begin to get a better handle on what these pitfalls look, sound, and feel like to you, over time you'll more quickly be able to recognize that you're headed toward a pitfall well before it's taken hold and created unintended consequences and negative effects.

In my case, thankfully I caught onto what was happening with the pitfalls with five months to spare on my publishing deadline. This allowed enough time to have a thoughtful conversation with my publisher to explain where I was and what I had learned, to ask for an extension, and to share how I was going to do things differently to meet the new deadline. The actions embedded in each of the five Ps also indicated what I needed to do to get back on track: realign with my purpose in writing the book, update my processes to create realistic work goals, reach out to people who could help and collaborate, cultivate the presence to stay focused and deal with the range of emotions I was experiencing, and, with peace, loosen my grip on the process and trust that I *would* create the manuscript I most hoped for.

The Leader You Feed and the Five Ps

As we become more aware of when Leader B has become the operating norm, and the triggers that cause us to slide down the slippery slope, we increase our ability to lift out of the noise and consider a different way of looking at things. We realize that every moment presents a choice between being Leader A and Leader B, and that we have the power to choose the course of action that will bring us back to Leader A.

The choice we have between Leader A and Leader B reminds me of a Cherokee Indian legend. Here is how this story goes.

A Cherokee elder was teaching his grandson about life. "A fight is going on inside me," he said to the boy. "It is a terrible fight and it is between two wolves. One is evil—he is anger, envy, sorrow, regret, greed, arrogance, self-pity, guilt, resentment, inferiority, lies, false pride, superiority, and ego. The other is good—he is joy, peace, love, hope, serenity, humility, kindness, benevolence, empathy, generosity, truth, compassion, and faith. The same fight is going on inside you—and inside every other person, too."

The grandson thought about it for a minute and then asked, "Grandfather, which wolf will win?"

The old Cherokee simply replied, "The one you feed."

To me this legend captures a profound truth: whatever we "feed," whatever we sustain with our time, energy, and action, is what will flourish. We can nurture and sustain an attitude of anger, arrogance, or inferiority, just as we can nurture and sustain an attitude of peace, empathy, or compassion. So it is with anything: what we feed is what will flourish.

How do we feed Leader A? The first step is built upon self-awareness, and this is where our inner spectator comes in. Knowing which wolf you are at the moment is a prerequisite to feeding the right one. We need to become a spectator to our own experience so we can recognize when we've fallen into Leader B mode and understand what led us there. Getting back to Leader A after you've been in Leader B mode requires the ability to "clean the lens" and take a larger, more elevated view from above the fray. It requires the willingness and the ability to come out of the trenches and regularly take stock of ourselves. As we mature and our self-awareness deepens, we will recognize more quickly when we start down the slippery slope and can arrest the slide well before entering a pitfall. We learn the particular set of factors that help us to be our most effective, present, and authentic selves.

FIGURE 1-2

From pitfalls to performance enhancers

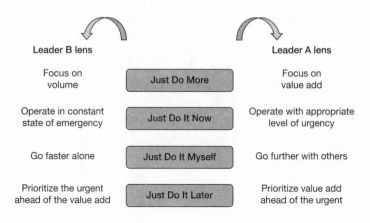

Leader B lens		Leader A lens
Focus on volume	Just Do More	Focus on value add
Operate in constant state of emergency	Just Do It Now	Operate with appropriate level of urgency
Go faster alone	Just Do It Myself	Go further with others
Prioritize the urgent ahead of the value add	Just Do It Later	Prioritize value add ahead of the urgent

When we continually feed Leader A and can habitually look at life through the Leader A lens, we can even turn a pitfall into a performance enhancer. Take a look at how it can work.

The Leader A lens allows a kind of alchemy to happen. I'll Just Do More becomes "I'll do more only if they are things that add value." I'll Just Do It Now shifts to "I'll do it now only after weighing each decision and determining that the task is truly urgent and in my wheelhouse." I'll Just Do It Myself becomes "I'll do it myself only if it's my highest and best use and it benefits the team and organization." And finally, I'll Just Do It Later becomes "I'll do it later only after assessing the situation and making a conscious decision to de-prioritize a project or a task."

The good news is, we don't have to do any of this work alone. Attending to the five Ps provides a methodical framework for remaining in Leader A mode as much as we can, and for feeding our good wolf after slipping into Leader B mode or even a full-blown pitfall. The five Ps, in fact, are a reliable antidote to each of the pitfalls—they give us confidence that there is a way to get back on track, and when regularly attended to, they enhance our overall performance. As often as we need to, we can align and realign ourselves to the five Ps.

Leader A stays connected to *purpose* and regularly infuses it into her day-to-day. She upgrades her *processes* as needed to execute her highest and best work. Leader A relies on the *people* around him—he creates an invigorated and effective team and a strong community of support. Leader A has a *presence* that is calm, stays focused, and doesn't react impulsively. And ultimately, like the tale of the two wolves, Leader A is able to be at *peace*, leading from a place of generosity, humility, and servant leadership rather than from striving, greed, false pride, or ego. He knows that a mix of Leader A and Leader B is all part of the entire leadership experience, and he can put *all* of it to work for the greater good.

It's time to begin. Our first leg of the journey introduces us to the first P, *purpose*, which undergirds and threads through every moment of leadership we'll encounter.

What to Remember:

> All leaders fluctuate between Leader A and Leader B mode. The key is to recognize when our lens begins to shift from Leader A to Leader B, and to become aware of the triggers that start us down the slippery slope to Leader B.

> Once we're on the slippery slope, we risk falling into one or more of the Four Pitfalls of Doing, which keep us locked in a cycle of stress, ineffectiveness, negativity, and feeling overwhelmed: I'll Just Do More Pitfall, I'll Just Do It Now Pitfall, I'll Just Do It Myself Pitfall, and I'll Just Do It Later Pitfall.

> As we become more in tune with ourselves, we become increasingly able to lift out of the noise and consider a different way of looking at things. We realize that every moment presents a choice between Leader A and Leader B, and that we can choose the course of action that brings us back to Leader A.

> Habitually feeding Leader A allows us to turn any pitfall into a performance enhancer. The five-P framework gives us a way to keep feeding Leader A, and to align and realign ourselves to these principles of effective leadership as often as we need to.

CHAPTER TWO

The Power of Purpose

Reset Your Compass

W hen I met Kate, the first thing I noticed was the sheer exhaustion in her eyes. You could sense the stress simmering just beneath the professional mask. Kate was clearly stretched too thin, and I wondered how long she'd be able to keep up with the demands she was facing.

Kate was a newly minted partner in a consulting firm and already finding herself falling into the I'll Just Do More Pitfall. After years of excellent client work on engagements, she was now also responsible for leading firm-level initiatives, and she was playing a larger role in recruiting. Her compensation was now tied more closely to her ability to drive business development and sell work. As Kate had to wear more hats than ever before, her stress levels steadily climbed, and she wondered if she could keep up with the demands of being a partner. The tipping point arrived when a trusted peer pulled her aside to let her know about the talk around the office: others noticed she was becoming increasingly defensive in meetings, especially when colleagues brought a different approach or perspective to the table.

Over the course of a six-month coaching engagement, I came to know Kate as a person of the highest integrity—she had a core value of intellectual honesty and rigor that I admired. I also came to appreciate her witty sense of humor, which shined when she was well rested and less stressed. We especially connected because we were both working moms, trying to grow professionally while also taking care of our families. Part of our work together was exploring what made for Kate's best days, when she was operating out of a Leader A mindset, and what conditions were in play when she felt defensive and found herself responding to colleagues in a Leader B way. It was clear from the outset that Kate was in a high-stress, high-responsibility position in her new officer-level role, where she had to produce, manage, and lead all at the same time. And on days when it felt as if she did nothing but attend to fire drills with absolutely no time to focus or get anything meaningful completed, her stress became unmanageable.

Then one morning, Kate came to a coaching meeting looking cheerful and more relaxed. With a glimmer in her eye, she declared, "I finally got it."

She went on to describe a metaphor that even years later still stands out for me. "I realized I'm always chopping wood," she said. "And my answer to everything is to chop *more* wood. When I'm stressed out, I just do more and fill my day with activity, emails, any interruption that comes along, firefighting. But today, I woke up and asked myself a different question: Is there a better way to chop this wood? Should I be chopping this wood at all?"

Kate realized she was stuck in a vicious cycle. When her stress level went up, she responded with the I'll Just Do More Pitfall: completing a litany of lower-priority tasks gave her a temporary sense of relief as she blazed through actionable items on a to-do list. But all that "chopping wood" was actually causing more stress, and it had her stuck in a grind of tasks that was obscuring her highest and best use at work and draining her of enthusiasm and energy. When Kate felt she was doing nothing but chopping wood, she got defensive.

Kate had made a major breakthrough in realizing that she responded to stress by creating . . . more stress. When we're in the I'll Just Do More Pitfall and Leader B has become more of the operating norm, it can feel like we're always chopping wood. We're working tirelessly but the wood just keeps accumulating—to no clear end or purpose. It's easy, in the stress of intense jobs and heavy workloads, to lose sight of what we're working toward. Or why we're even chopping so much wood in the first place.

The Impact of Purpose on Leader A and Leader B

Kate's story is a reminder of just how easy it is to let the day-to-day whirlwind and the increasing complexity of our roles make us feel out of control and slip into Leader B mode. As one client described it, "Somehow it feels like you've been ejected from the driver's seat and the world is driving *you*." It's at these moments that you might find yourself asking questions such as:

- Does the portfolio of work I'm responsible for allow me to use my gifts and make a difference? Does it include things that are important to me?

- Am I doing this for the right reasons?

- Why am I doing this in the first place?

There's a quote from an unknown source that I've always loved: "What comes first, the compass or the clock? Before one can truly manage time (the clock), it is important to know where you are going, what your priorities and goals are, in which direction you are headed (the compass). Where you are headed is more important than how fast you are going. Rather than always focusing on what's urgent, learn to focus on what is really important."

What's really important—"the compass," or our purpose—is the focus of this chapter. Getting grounded in our purpose at work gives us a greater sense of control and can go a long way in lifting us out of that day-to-day grind Kate was experiencing. With greater clarity in our purpose, the compass can guide the clock.

In this chapter we're going to bring greater focus to purpose— a notoriously amorphous concept. You'll learn to make purpose more concrete by using what I call the "purpose = contribution + passion" equation. I'll share a tool called the purpose quadrants to manage your time, your energy, and your career. And finally, we'll look at the reality of daily demands and learn how to most effectively triage and sift our yesses and nos in a way that's based on our purpose.

Use the "Purpose = Contribution + Passion" Equation

We all want a sense of purpose, an awareness that we're doing our highest and best work and that our work has meaning and is making a difference. But let's just acknowledge from the outset that conversations on purpose can be as frustrating as they are enticing. Some of my clients have described having "an allergic reaction" to even thinking about purpose because the concept is so abstract and hard to pin down—difficult to talk about, much less define and identify. Others are disappointed and frustrated that they haven't yet found their purpose. Still others, like Kate, are so overextended it feels as if the last thing they have the time (or patience) for is pondering the whys and wherefores of their existence.

This is why I counsel folks to cut themselves some slack and begin by getting grounded in two important components of purpose: contribution and passion. Below is a simple equation that can help you get clearer on your purpose at work and make the whole idea of purpose more concrete and accessible.

Purpose = your contribution + your passion

Contribution: Define the Tangible and Intangible Elements

The first part of the purpose equation is your contribution. Contribution is about the value you're adding, the impact you're having, and the difference you're making. It's best captured in the simple question: What is your highest and best use?

There are both tangible and intangible elements of your contribution. The tangible aspects are clearly delineated, metric-driven, and measurable. They can include your:

- TECHNICAL OR FUNCTIONAL EXPERTISE: These are areas where you have command of a set of knowledge, facts, answers, data, or skills. Often you are on a team or in a role so you can share and bring this technical or functional expertise to bear.

- DELIVERABLES: These are items you deliver to teams and the organization. They could include analyses, documents, memos, products, systems, and plans.

- RESULTS: Ultimately, the most tangible metrics track our results. All businesses and functions have these metrics captured in functional plans, scorecards, or dashboards. At the highest level of an organization, results are most often reflected in the P&L and the entity's financial results.

The intangible aspects of contribution are less concrete, but they become increasingly important as you take on larger or more senior roles in an organization. They include:

- THOUGHT LEADERSHIP AND STRATEGY: I'm not talking about just vision or strategy but your ability in any interaction or conversation to see the big picture, exercise business judgment, connect the dots, see around corners, lay out alternatives, articulate risks and trade-offs, or present organizing frameworks that help make the complex simpler.

- INFLUENCE: Most work today in organizational life requires working with many people and many different types of people. Leaders must be able to win the hearts and minds of others in order to drive and lead change. Influence includes the ability to articulate and paint a vision for others and know how to effectively enroll and bring others along. As one CEO shared with me, being a CEO isn't about just making decisions and handing those down to others—it's

ultimately about influencing others to want to do those
things with a lot of energy and motivation.

- PRESENCE: The ripple effect you have on the organization
matters. As the leader you are the model for the entire team,
and there's no off switch for that. Recall how Kate was
telegraphing stress, which was starting to impact others
negatively. As a leader in her firm, her Leader B days carried
greater ramifications than when she was less senior.

- VISIBILITY: The networks and people with whom we come in
contact form another intangible contribution as we help
spread the good word about our work throughout the
organization, or perhaps externally to customers or other key
stakeholders. This can include helping in sourcing efforts,
board meetings, or recruiting. Additionally, you may have
built a reputation, platform, or brand in the marketplace that
connects or brings in key relationships for your organization.

Passion: Define What Stokes Your Fire

The second part of the purpose equation is your passion. While
contribution is about action, *passion* is about the motivation, energy, and inspiration that fuels the action. If we think of contribution as our highest and best *use*, passion is our highest and best
juice.

Simply put, passion is what brings you inspiration, enjoyment,
and excitement in your work. It's something you alone can assess
and understand, and it's a critical component of purpose. You know
you're passionate about something when you find yourself wanting
to invest time and energy in it. It's what stokes your fire. In 2014, a
Deloitte study on workforce engagement found that "passionate
workers are committed to continually achieving higher levels of performance." They are the team members who "drive extreme and sustained performance improvement" and who help their organizations
grow stronger throughout any market challenge or disruption.[1]

Passionate people are inspired people, inherently motivated to
go the extra mile. Psychologist and author Scott Barry Kaufman

points out that inspiration "propels [us] from apathy to possibility, and transforms the way we perceive our own capabilities." As a group, inspired people tend to be more open to new experiences, and they report more absorption in their tasks, a stronger drive to master their work, and a host of positive psychological resources, including a belief in their own abilities, self-esteem, and optimism.[2] Ask yourself if *this* is how you feel when you go to work.

Let's return for a moment to Kate, who could hardly have felt less passionate or inspired about her work when we first met. To start getting her back into Leader A mode, we worked together on the purpose equation and used her answers to populate the contribution-passion table that follows. For Kate, the exercise

TABLE 2-1

The contribution-passion table

Areas of responsibility as partner in a consulting firm	Tangible contributions	Intangible contributions	Areas of passion
Business development	• Meet sales target for the year • Bring in $X in new client business development • Bring in $X in existing client accounts	• Win the hearts and minds of client management • Serve as a trusted advisor and thought partner to others	• The initial BD conversations, learning about the need and sharing about the firm • Don't enjoy the "BD operations components" and follow-through pieces; get team's help with this
Firm management and culture	• Lead committee for talent recruiting work	• Be a good sounding board to head of talent as partner on committee	• Leadership development and training—perhaps help to sponsor or host an event for up-and-coming talent
IP creation	• Publish two white papers this year for the firm	• Pull together and motivate research team on white paper	• Trends in AI
Client delivery	• Ensure scope of engagements is delivered well by teams	• Mentor and apprentice others	• Client meeting to review findings and recommendations

DO WHAT YOU'RE MADE FOR: WHAT THE ANCIENTS SAY ABOUT PURPOSE

One of my favorite quotes comes from the *Bhagavad Gita*, an ancient Hindu text that chronicles the struggle for self-mastery: "It is better to perform one's own duties imperfectly than to master the duties of another."[a]

Various translations render "duty," as "path," "occupation," or even "destiny," but in each case, this famous quote underscores the need for each of us to tend to and perform our own individual duties and not try to mold ourselves to someone else's path. Sometimes, the first step on the path to living and working out of your true purpose is identifying what you bring to the table that no one else can. This sounds obvious, but it's far easier said than done—especially when our organizations and managers aren't clear on identifying purpose for us or when we feel like we're living out someone else's ambition or dream for us.

In Eastern terms, you're not "living your dharma" if you're trying to be someone you're not. One's path or *dharma* has multiple meanings in various Eastern religions, and there is no single-word translation in Western languages. But one definition offers a description that I think is most relevant for leadership: "conformity to one's duty and nature."[b] We can think of living one's dharma as living and leading in a way that upholds one's unique duty and nature.

Let's break down this concept into leadership terms:

brought some immediate relief: she found that she gained significant clarity in lifting out of the day-to-day grind of "chopping wood" and gaining a more aerial view of the key parts of her contributions—the "big rocks," as she called them—as a new partner in the firm. Just as important was identifying which parts of this new job totally jazzed her. Kate and I plotted her answers as shown in table 2-1.

One key insight for Kate in this exercise was realizing that her contributions and passions hadn't always looked like this—and they would continue to change. At an earlier stage of her career,

- **DUTY** calls to mind the contributions we make each day at work and at home. In a leadership context, this word captures and reflects the value we add, the impact we generate, and the difference we make. *Duty* has a connotation of good citizenship and being in service of a greater purpose.

- **NATURE** points to the passion and motivation we experience when we tap into our innate talents, gifts, and preferences. You may have taken many assessments at this point in your career that give you greater clues to your unique nature and innate skills, such as CliftonStrengths Assessment (formerly known as the StrengthsFinder Assessment)®, MBTI®, Insights®, or DiSC®. These are the elements of your nature that make your leadership style different from anyone else's— and therefore uniquely valuable and indicative of your purpose.

- **CONFORMITY** to duty and nature could then be likened to the leadership word *alignment*. We could say that living your own "dharma leadership path" means that you've aligned your contributions (highest and best use) with your passions and interests (that which motivates you).

a. *The Bhagavad Gita*, 2nd ed., trans. Eknath Easwaran (Tomales, CA: Nilgiri Press, 2007), 253.
b. "Dharma," Merriam-Webster, https://www.merriam-webster.com/dictionary/dharma.

her first column would have been populated with individual client projects rather than broader areas of oversight. She also recognized how at an earlier stage it was actually easier to see and gauge her direct impact. Now, as a partner, her intangible contributions were more about the behaviors she modeled and how she influenced others directly and indirectly. Likewise for passion, she used to get jazzed about solving client problems and nailing an analysis, but now she found herself increasingly drawn to mentoring colleagues at earlier stages of their careers. This kind of exercise is especially important to complete when taking on a larger role or more responsibility, and can be useful to do even once a year.

Recognize That Purpose Is Dynamic and Ever-Evolving

Kate discovered that purpose isn't static and permanent, but rather dynamic and ever-evolving. This is a crucial concept—one that comes as a surprise to many folks. As much as we may like it to be, purpose isn't a single, permanent mandate the lucky few discover or have presented to them. It is a dynamic, ever-changing sense of being in alignment with your *current* highest and best use (contribution) as well as your *current* highest and best juice (passion).

Sometimes, our natural desire for a single, simple answer to the question of our purpose can actually hinder our ability to find the very thing we're seeking. But rather than a static, fixed thing that's somewhere "out there," waiting to be discovered, the more helpful and generative way to think about purpose is as an inner certitude that evolves over time and in response to different contexts and circumstances. And quite practically speaking, as a leader you simply can't operate in the same way you once did as you take on expanded and increasingly complex roles.

One former client, who is now the CEO of a health-care company, said if he had to identify one key element of his career success, it was realizing early on that every new role in his career carried its own particular purpose. Whether the new role came from a promotion or from a move to a different organization, his first task was always to get very clear on the mandate for the new role. He put it this way: "What is the reason I exist in *this* particular job?" Ironically, some of the most successful, capable people in the world find themselves mired in Leader B mode after they receive a promotion—not unlike what happened to Kate. Often, this is because they're still trying to live and work from their former purpose, when what's needed is revised purpose for their current role.

In his commencement address to the 2017 graduating class of his alma mater, Harvard University, Facebook CEO Mark Zuckerberg dispelled the idea that we must have a stable, once-and-for-all answer to the question of our purpose. Instead, he explained, purpose reveals itself to us gradually as we regularly engage with the things that both spark our inspiration (passion) and channel the impact (contribution) we hope to make in the world. The expectation that somehow we discover our purpose in "a single eureka moment," said Zuckerberg, "is a dangerous lie." Instead, he assured the grads, "ideas don't come out fully formed. They only become clear as you work on them."[3] Likewise, it may take a little effort to become acquainted with your new purpose at each new stage of your career development, but with the purpose equation, you'll always have an anchor.

Use the Purpose Quadrants to Manage Time and Energy

One of the best parts of making purpose more concrete is that you can then use it to manage your time and energy more intentionally and effectively. You can do this by taking both components of purpose we have discussed so far, your contribution and your passion, and create a 2×2 organizing framework that I call the *purpose quadrants*.

With contribution along the x axis and passion along the y axis, the purpose quadrants become a practical tool that accounts for your energy and motivation, as well as a way to categorize the litany of demands you face each day. Let's first look at what each quadrant houses, what it feels like within each one, and ultimately the actions you can take within each quadrant. Then you'll have a chance to create your own 2×2 purpose quadrants. Figure 2-1 gives you a quick description of each quadrant.

FIGURE 2-1

The 2×2 purpose quadrants

		Contribution (value add for org/role)	
		Low/unclear	High
Passion (value add to you)	High	**Quadrant III: Elevate** Either elevate the idea others don't understand the value of yet or elevate yourself, even if it's a task or activity you like or are good at. Know when you've hit the tipping point	**Quadrant I: Prioritize** Prioritize the items, tasks, and activities where the highest contribution to the organization and your passion match
	Low	**Quadrant IV: Delegate, hire, or eliminate** Delegate, hire for, or eliminate items in this box altogether	**Quadrant II: Tolerate** Tolerate the things you'll never love about the job or things that you're on a learning curve for now but impact your long-term contribution. Know when you've hit the tipping point

Quadrant I: Prioritize

What it is: This is the sweet spot of your job. Items in Quadrant I reflect the highest value for your contributions as well as your highest passion. These are the parts of your job that bring you energy, joy, and impact, and this is where you're most likely to feel a sense of purpose and that you're making a difference.

What it feels like: The leaders who are living and leading out of their sense of purpose are the ones who are most often operating out of QI, and they're the ones who enjoy a higher proportion of Leader A days. I've noticed that these clients even describe their best days in remarkably similar language. Words such as *high impact, effortless, made a difference, motivated, in the zone, fired up,* and *authentic* come up time and again. As a coach, this is the kind of outcome I want for everyone I work with—to spend more of their time and energy in Quadrant I, where there is a higher likelihood of deriving a sense of motivation, effectiveness, meaning, and success.

Key actions: The action steps for Quadrant I are clear: as much as possible, *prioritize* and make time for those items. I often advise clients to pick a color to code on their calendars for QI so they can always see how often they're making these activities or initiatives a top priority. Chapter 3 on process will go into more detail about how you can color-code to keep track of QI, given its importance to ensuring your time is focused and that you are regularly re-charged and energized by your job.

Quadrant II: Tolerate

What it is: We won't love every part of the job, even some of the parts where we're making the highest contribution, or the contribution our organization, boss, or key stakeholders most value. These are parts of our role that we know are important but don't exactly inspire us. In some cases, these parts of the job never did inspire us, and in other cases, we've become bored with them or have outgrown them.

What it feels like: These are parts of the role that are important but drain your energy when you're engaging in them. You might find yourself resisting, avoiding, or putting off these things. However you react, there's some level of discomfort when you are engaging in a Quadrant II item or activity. You often think, if I just didn't have to do this part of my job . . .

Key action: The key action in Quadrant II is to *tolerate* these sets of activities or, where possible, delegate, hire, or outsource. Often, building a team around you with complementary interests and skills can be key to fulfilling your highest and best use while preserving your own inspiration and juice. But there's one key caveat: only tolerate if your role still affords you plenty of Quadrant I tasks and responsibilities. If you find yourself spending most of your days in QII, then read ahead in chapter 2 to learn how to use the purpose quadrants to manage transitions in your career.

For example, one CEO of a startup couldn't figure out why she was feeling so drained and listless. She loved the vision and mission of her organization, and she felt she was made for this job. She'd even recently secured funding that would make her vision a greater reality. Understandably, she was perplexed as to why she wasn't feeling excited about work.

I suggested we use the 2×2 to figure out what was going on. We started by defining her top three to five contributions for the year. Then, we talked about the kinds of things she was most passionate about.

In laying out her 2×2, the answer to the energy-drain question suddenly became clear. For this executive, fund-raising was in Quadrant I. It was a part of the role she most enjoyed—being out on the road, pitching and selling her ideas, networking, and raising capital. But now with fund-raising behind her, she was immersed in more detailed-oriented and operational parts of the business that were in her Quadrant II.

Until she could make a key hire who could take over some of those tasks, she'd be in the trenches on some things she was less excited about. But it was a huge relief to know why she was feeling drained—and to know this state was temporary until she made that hire. She could now see how part of being a leader of a growing startup was tolerating the gap that can arise between growth in infrastructure and lagging resources.

We discussed how in the meantime she could anchor in the bigger vision she held for the company whenever she had to engage in those QII activities. It helped enormously to connect back to her overall purpose and remember why she was doing these things. Leaning on purpose goes a long way in getting you through the inevitable dips and valleys of work.

Quadrant III: Elevate

What it is: You might find there are parts of the job that you really love, but other people don't see these things as your highest contribution. The passion is there but the value is unclear.

What it feels like: These are parts of the role that give you a lot of energy and that you enjoy engaging in; however, you know these are not things your boss or others would say are the best use of your time. That said, you still find yourself saying yes to them or making time for them because these tasks stoke your fire.

Key action: Quadrant III may be a signal that it's time to *elevate* the value of your idea, task, or activity. Perhaps you see a hot new area, but the impact isn't yet apparent to others. It may be time to share and road-show what you're seeing out on the horizon that fuels your conviction, and make the case for why it's good not only for you but also for the organization.

QIII can also be a signal to elevate yourself. Be mindful of areas that you still enjoy—perhaps from a previous role or from when the company was smaller—but that really aren't your highest contribution anymore. Maybe you love to fix problems and have a bias toward action, which leads you to get involved in things your team should be handling. With this knowledge in place, you can hit pause before diving in.

Quadrant IV: Delegate, Hire, or Eliminate

What it is: This quadrant is about chopping wood. Quadrant IV is where we get caught up in the churn of activities that are lower value and don't produce energy, leaving us on the way to burnout.

What it feels like: This is a funny quadrant because on the one hand, like Kate in our opening example, it can create a temporary sense of relief to cross easy things off the list. Over time, however, it drains our energy because on some level, we know the "big rocks" and important things aren't being attended to. We know that we're ultimately not making the difference we hope to make, and we're not enjoying what we're doing.

Key action: Where possible, *delegate* or outsource these activities or make the case for a new hire. The ideal scenario is that your Quadrant IV is someone else's Quadrant I (see chapter 4 on people for more on this). If a resource just isn't possible at this time, be careful attending to these items during key windows of time where your highest energy is better spent on critical-path QI items, in which case you should *deprioritize* them.

QIV, however, is a good quadrant to pay attention to because the items you list in QIV can give you clues as to what is wrong in your job, and more insight into what to do about it. One professional, Jorge, loved his job, but lately was feeling stressed and less motivated than before. One project in particular became the focus of his thoughts at work and at home, and it seemed to cast a dark cloud over his entire work experience—even though his other projects were going well. I asked him to use the 2×2 to track and compare this project that felt so draining against another one that was going particularly well.

What he found was that with the current project, many of the tasks he was assigned were in Quadrant IV: he didn't like doing them, and he didn't feel like he was adding the value he hoped to. There were so many people on the team, it was hard to find a lane that was his to own.

With greater clarity around what was wrong, Jorge decided to take two actions. First, he spoke to his project lead about how he could find ways to increase his tangible contribution to the team. And he realized that rather than just focusing on finding what "more" he could do (and risk falling into the I'll Just Do More Pitfall), he also wanted to think about his intangible contributions and perhaps derive more passion by mentoring some of the more junior members of the team. The 2×2 helped him zero in on what was actually wrong, which gave him a way to articulate his concerns and a set of actions to take.

EXERCISE

What's in Your Quadrants?

Take a stab at setting up your own purpose quadrants. To do so, refer back to the definitions of contribution and passion in the previous section, or you can use the following questions to guide you.

1. First, create a list of your tangible and intangible contributions for the *x* axis. You can ask yourself questions such as:

   – What is my highest and best use?

   – What would my boss say is my highest and best use?

   – What would my direct reports say?

   – What would my peers say?

   – What would customers/clients say?

   Contribution must be considered thoughtfully. It includes your own definition of the difference you want to make, what value you add, and the impact you intend to have, but it also includes the viewpoints of others. Often, we underestimate what our highest contribution really is. So how would your boss, peers, direct reports, executive team, customers, or board describe the difference you are making, the value you are adding, and the impact you're having? If you don't feel you have a good read on what others believe and perceive about you, don't be shy about asking them directly for this input. You can do this at the start of the year or during a one-on-one, or have a leadership coach solicit this kind of information during a 360-review process. Be on the lookout for times when there is a disconnect between your own view of your best and highest use and that of your colleagues, especially your boss.

2. Create a second list for the *y* axis of the purpose quadrants that captures the items you feel the most intrinsic motivation and energy toward in your current role. These are the things that inspire you or excite you most, the things you really look forward to doing. You can ask yourself the following questions:

   – What is my highest and best juice?

   – Where do I want to spend time and invest emotional energy?

   – What is it I want to be learning?

   – What stokes my fire now?

– What gives me energy, motivation, and inspiration?

3. Now, look at both lists you've created and put a star next to anything that shows up on both.

4. Look at all your starred items and transfer them into Q1 in figure 2-2.

5. Look at your non-starred items from your contributions list and transfer them into Q2.

6. Look at your non-starred items from your passion list and transfer them into Q3.

7. Now, write down any other activities or tasks from your current role that are not on any of your lists into Q4.

8. As you look at your quadrants, how does this information help you better understand your current level of motivation and energy?

9. What actions or changes will you make as a result of this information?

FIGURE 2-2

What's in your quadrants?

	Contribution (value add for org/role)	
	Low/unclear	High
Passion (value add to you) — High	Quadrant III	Quadrant I
Passion (value add to you) — Low	Quadrant IV	Quadrant II

Use the Purpose Quadrants to Manage Transitions in Your Career

In addition to prioritizing your time and energy, the purpose quadrants are also a great way to manage transitions in your career. Both Quadrants II and III can signal that it could be time for a career move or a change in role.

Watch Out for the Boredom Signal

Boredom is a very important warning sign that you've started to outgrow your role. You know you are still contributing and making the impact your organization wants you to make, but you don't have any passion. You spend a lot of time on Quadrant II tasks. You find yourself bored and restless and starting to stagnate.

One of my clients realized it was time to look for new roles or even a new job because as he mapped out his 2×2, he found that almost everything in his existing role was in the lower-right quadrant, QII. He was stunned to find that he was merely tolerating 90 percent of his current role! He also discovered he was taking on tasks that his boss said weren't in his lane or weren't important, and he was starting to spend more time in QIII as a result.

He realized from looking at his purpose quadrants that it was time to start having conversations with his boss to see about future roles or new projects that might reignite his passion and boost his interest level. He was ready for something new and interesting and, in many ways, had simply outgrown his current job. The 2×2 exercise revealed it was time to make changes.

Watch Out for the Misalignment Signal

In Quadrant III, you might recognize there are things you're still doing that you enjoy but no longer fit your highest and best use. Or perhaps you've been trying to get your boss or team to see the value in a new idea you're passionate about, and you realize that your ideas are falling on deaf ears and you'll never get the chance to make your vision a reality.

Either way, this quadrant signals that there is a growing disconnect between what keeps you motivated and what your organization values. Ultimately, if this continues to happen, it may be time to move on. Christine Day, in a 2014 interview with *Fortune*, said she knew it was time to leave Lululemon as CEO when her vision for the company no longer matched the founder's. "You have to take control of your own life and say, 'This isn't working for me,'" she said. In her next leadership role, she teamed up with a health food company because she was "captured by the mission."[4] She found alignment between her passions and the organization's mission and values.

USING THE PURPOSE QUADRANTS AT HOME AND IN EVERYDAY LIFE

You can extend the 2x2 exercise beyond work. I've found it helpful in prioritizing time and energy at home, too. Each year I sit down with my son and ask him the top three things I do as a mom that he values most. I want to know which of my contributions matter most in his mind. As a full-time working parent, this is a critical conversation. You can't be all things to all people.

Then, I line up his top three against what inspires me or gives me passion as a parent. I aim for the upper-right quadrant (Quadrant I), where purpose feels most alive, and I stay in touch with what that means now. It's been amazing to see how the items in QI have evolved and will continue to do so as my son hits different stages and ages. One year, we found great overlap between his view of contribution and my passion, which included hosting playdates, making his school lunch, and reading him bedtime stories. As he's gotten older, the new top three include dropping him off at school, taking him to karate practice, and being at volleyball tournaments.

This also provides part of the "family compass" around which we build our home and work schedules, and it teaches my son how to prioritize.

Use Purpose for Sifting Everyday Demands and Requests

While the purpose quadrants give us clarity on where to prioritize our time and energy, the reality is that most days are made up of small decisions about where to focus our time and energy. To stay out of Leader B mode, it's important to connect with your purpose to help you to sift through the many demands and requests of a given day.

Sift Your Yesses and Nos through the Contribution and Passion Filter

Every day we're bombarded with meeting invites, requests from other people, and the overall barrage of logistics and activity. Before automatically saying yes or no to any requests, hit the pause button and keep your upper-right quadrant (Quadrant I) in mind.

Meeting Requests. One of the challenges I know almost every leader grapples with is the litany of meetings we find ourselves in—surely one of the hallmarks of today's organizational life. We've all had days when every hour is taken up in back-to-back meetings, with absolutely no white space on the calendar. Granted, there is some portion of this that may not be in your control, but when I've pushed clients to really question the necessity of some of these meetings, or the timing or urgency of them because of someone else's need or anxiety, far more often than not we've been able to recover some space on their calendars.

At the start of the week or day, look at the meeting invites on your calendar and use the following questions to sift your yes or no. The aim is to ensure that you get at least one component of purpose fulfilled by attending each meeting.

- CONTRIBUTION: Is this a meeting I will add value to if I attend?

- PASSION: Is this a meeting I will derive value from by attending?

- IMPACT: What is the impact if I go or don't go?

- POSSIBLE ACTION: Is there someone else who can go in my place?

One leader shared with me how liberating it was to respectfully move meetings, push them out, or even decline them altogether without the consequences he thought it would bring. In fact, he was surprised when a few of his colleagues said they were happy to get some "bonus free time" back, too. This leader also found over the long run that his yesses to attend a meeting meant more. His new definition of a yes became: he truly felt he should be there, he would add *and* derive value, and he would be 100 percent present.

Extracurricular Requests. As you gain more influence, you might receive an increasing number of requests to attend dinners, join boards, speak at events, or be a mentor. All these activities are great and can feel flattering, but they take time and energy. Consider each request against your purpose (contribution + passion), as opposed to obligation or guilt.

- CONTRIBUTION: Is this something where I can uniquely add value?

- PASSION: Is this something I will derive value from by attending or joining?

- IMPACT: How does this align with my larger purpose and vision?

The reality is you can't do it all. Often, you will be asked to attend an event or join a cause, but it's not the right time to take it on. One working parent shared with me how she felt conflicted about joining the board of her son's school. She wanted to be involved in supporting his education, and moreover, she felt a sense of obligation because it seemed like all her colleagues sat on their children's school boards. The position also brought a certain level of prestige in her community. The more we explored the issue, however, the more it became clear that taking on this role felt like work; she had a full-time job that required lots of planning and leadership skills, and understandably, she wanted a break when she wasn't working.

Ultimately, she made the decision not to join the board. Instead, she chose to reserve her time and energy for high-interaction activities with her son where she felt she could make the kind of difference she wanted to and that brought her the most energy. She carved out time to be a chaperone for some of his school trips, when she was actually with him. She didn't let a "should" or a "it sounds good on paper" cause her to fall into the I'll Just Do More Pitfall. Instead, she was honest with herself and got really clear on what was important to her and what worked best for her family.

Work Requests. Obviously at work, you have less latitude on yesses and nos, but even then, don't let the habit of saying yes automatically guide your decisions. Instead, organize your yesses into three buckets:

- THE STRATEGIC YES: Some requests are of high strategic importance and excite you, so they squarely fit in your Quadrant I. These are strategic yesses. Sometimes, however, you may find that a strategic yes also lives in Quadrant II—you recognize that someone of higher authority, influence, or power is asking and that you don't have the leeway to say no. It requires some political savvy to read the tea leaves for these situations. In these cases, it's about saying yes, and then optimizing how you carry out the tasks without getting drained.

- THE PARTIAL YES: These are requests that have some importance, and you determine you want to be involved in some way. But you also recognize that you don't have to sign up for the whole thing and that there is room to negotiate. The best-case scenario occurs when you seize the opportunity to be the trusted advisor or thought partner on a request. This is especially important because often your boss or your client may ask for something in a way that makes you feel like you have to jump through hoops immediately and fall into the I'll Just Do More or I'll Just Do It Now Pitfalls. However, if what they are asking for doesn't make strategic sense or you think there is a better way to do it, then have a conversation that acknowledges their need but helps get to a better solution.

- IT'S NOT ACTUALLY MY YES: Watch out for those requests or situations that are not actually "yours to own" or that don't need to become your responsibility. Look for places where you might be enabling others because you always take care of others or rescue others. In these cases, help redirect them to the right person or resource. (See chapter 4 on people to understand more about upgrading your boundaries and rules of engagement with others.)

Work Products. You can sift for contribution and passion even down to the work-product level. If you find yourself working on a deliverable that isn't super high in contribution or passion but you're putting in a high amount of effort and energy, ask yourself if your quest to be perfect is worth it.

Places to watch out for include spending inordinate time on presentations, crossing every *i* and dotting every *t*, overengineering a process, or staying in the weeds on a task or initiative too long—all at the expense of the higher-order contribution on a given deliverable. As your leadership role grows, it's likely you won't have the bandwidth to spend so much time and energy at a granular level. Your expanded role likely requires that you think at a more strategic level, or spend time engaging in important conversations with others on the topic or issue at hand.

A Final Word on Purpose

I love when I see others infuse more purpose into their lives. They begin to feel like they're spending more time making the difference they'd hoped to make or that they're adding more value, or they just feel fired up by what they're working on. Busy days aren't likely to disappear from our lives, but I continue to aspire for all of us to have "good-busy" days. This is what it feels like to live and lead with a Leader A mindset.

As your compass becomes clearer and you begin to align your time, energy, career, and yesses and nos to that compass, you'll find that at the highest level you are starting to *say yes to yourself* more often. Making this shift can be hard at first, but it does give you the opportunity to tap into your inner wells of courage and your convictions about what matters most. It shows you how to channel your efforts and motivation into the things with the highest impact and the highest inspiration.

Purpose-governed living can require a shift in your thinking, but it is worth the effort. Living out of your purpose ultimately results in more courageous, confident, and effective leadership. And a more fulfilled and satisfied you.

What to Remember:

> ➤ The purpose P is a critical part of a leader's overall long-term effectiveness and satisfaction. It's easy to let the day-to-day whirlwind and increasing complexity of our roles lead us to feeling out of control. Come back to feeding Leader A by resetting your compass with purpose. You can do this by using the purpose equation (purpose = your contributions + your passions) to make purpose more concrete, using the purpose quadrants for managing time, energy, and your career, and more effectively sifting your yesses and nos.

> ➤ Purpose doesn't have to be abstract and hard to pin down. Be concrete about your contribution and passion. They serve as vital markers that keep us anchored in our purpose over time.

> ➤ You can use the purpose quadrants to concretely plot your contributions and passions, creating an organizing framework to manage your time and energy more effectively. You can take more decisive and strategic action by seeing what parts of your job fit within the 2×2 quadrants. The quadrants

also offer a way to manage career transitions by helping you notice and pay special attention to boredom and misalignment signals.

➤ Even amid busy days when you're bombarded with meeting invites, requests from other people, and a barrage of work products you have to complete, you can still stay connected to your purpose by keeping contribution and passion in your mind as you better and more strategically sift your yesses and nos.

➤ As many ancient traditions describe, purpose ultimately keeps us on our own authentic path, doing what we're made for rather than living by another person's desire, agenda, or expectations. Continue to tap into your natural courage and conviction to say yes to yourself and to the difference and impact you hope to make now, which inspires your imagination and stokes your fire.

CHAPTER THREE

The Power of Process
Reboot Your Personal Operating System

I met Thomas, a marketing leader, when his enthusiasm for his job was at an all-time high. He loved his work and the entrepreneurial spirit of his company, and he was very excited by its rapid growth and transformation. A passionate, visionary, and creative leader, Thomas brought an informal style to the role that colleagues loved; one of his strengths was being able to connect with others in a fluid and personable way. His shoot-from-the-hip approach and bias to action were a big part of the company's success to date.

Thomas's concern was that he didn't want to stall out as he had seen happen to other leaders who weren't able to scale their capacity and abilities when their companies scaled. He really wanted to keep up, but during this period of rapid transformation, he already felt pulled and stretched in many directions, and he feared he was slipping out of Leader A mode.

While Thomas thrived under high-pressure, competitive situations, he was starting to experience the downsides of the Just Do It Now Pitfall as the sheer volume, pace, and intensity of his role grew. He felt like he was rushing from one meeting to the next, without having time to work on the things that mattered most. Digital marketing, big data, and the increasing number of platforms to reach customers were changing his industry and company quickly, and the executive team was anxious to make sure the company was keeping up with trends in marketing analytics and data. This added even more pressure.

Thomas was able to keep pace on both the day-to-day work and the larger projects that mattered most to the company's growth—but sometimes just barely, and he felt increasingly drained and less present. Some of his team members had even expressed concern about how on edge he seemed.

When Thomas and I met, he already had an accurate read on his situation. As he put it, he and his company were "on eerily similar growth paths," and he realized they both needed to implement more formal processes and structures to get to the next level. Thomas's challenge was to preserve his entrepreneurial spirit and informal leadership style while upgrading his own processes to ensure that he continued to stay as effective as possible in a larger context and environment.

The Impact of Process on Leader A and Leader B

Thomas is not unlike top athletes, dedicated artists, and even Buddhist monks. What's the common thread? Each knows that being committed to a set of daily processes, practices, and rituals supports their most effective way of being in the world.

Consider the 2017 Super Bowl in which the New England Patriots played against the Atlanta Falcons. The Falcons were leading by a score of 28–3 in the third quarter when the game took a turn. As things started to fall apart for the Falcons, the Patriots began to gain momentum and the game went into overtime. The Patriots came back to win the Super Bowl, giving legendary quarterback Tom Brady the fifth Super Bowl win of his career.

Just two days before the game, Tom Brady was featured on the NPR podcast *On Point* on an episode entitled "How Aging Athletes Continue to Win Big." Brady, who was thirty-nine at the time of Super Bowl LI, is well known for his strict fitness and nutrition regimen, and during the interview he detailed the set of rituals and processes he relies on for staying in top shape. The podcast also featured tennis superstars Serena Williams and Roger Federer, who like Brady have played well beyond the age of most athletes in their sport. These athletes have found ways to stay in tune with themselves as they age, resetting their processes as necessary to support their longevity as champions.

Many sports stars' pregame rituals—which may seem bizarre to the outside observer—are just as much a part of their process. Serena Williams is known to wear the same pair of socks throughout a tournament, tie her shoes the same way each time she laces up, and bounce the ball exactly five times before her first serve. Despite her prodigious skill and countless hours of practice, she's blamed losses on not following this routine. And she's hardly alone. Sports enthusiasts ranging from world-class athletes to weekend warriors rely on their own set of rituals and practices—tapping the bat on the toe of a cleat or wearing a lucky shirt, for example, to give themselves an edge. It's easy to dismiss such actions as superstition, but research has shown that these rituals actually work because they reduce tension and give a player a sense of control and confidence in a high-stakes, anxiety-provoking situation.[1] It's that increased calm and confidence that positively impacts performance.

Though Buddhist monks and artists may seem to be at the opposite end of the spectrum when it comes to the rigors of following their chosen path, neither path is possible without a commitment to process. For practitioners of modalities such as yoga and meditation, daily rituals and practices are the very bedrock of existence. And dedicated artists must put in the work every day—not just when the mood strikes them or when inspiration arrives.

Whether it's an athlete, a monk, an artist, or an individual leader, the reality is that the second P, *process*, is a key part of supporting Leader A. In a world where it can feel like there are never enough hours in the day for all that we need to get done, our daily practices and routines can enhance performance, save time, help us restore, and provide critical guardrails. They can give us a much-needed sense of choice and agency in the face of what can feel like an overwhelming workload and a hectic pace. Some leaders describe this second P as their safety net—their processes provide a sense of security and prevent them from going into a free fall—while others think of it as basic "hygiene," or practices they do every single day to keep themselves on point. Still others think of the whole set of their practices and routines as their personal operating system. I think that's an apt image, because it captures the system-wide need for process—and reminds us that much like our laptops and smartphones, our personal operating system will need periodic upgrades.

There are four components of a leader's personal operating system that can help us feed Leader A or get back on track quickly when slipping into a string of Leader B days. We'll look at each in this chapter. I'll start by asking you a series of questions so you can better understand your context and preferences and ensure that your processes are designed for and aligned with who you are and what supports your highest and best self. Second, we'll look at the processes and structures that protect your time for what matters most. Then, I'll share practices that ensure you are recharging your energy. Finally, we'll end by putting it all together, and I'll show you how you can apply the concepts in this chapter to have sound rituals to use when you're on the road.

Design Processes That Fit You and Your Context

Because each of us is unique, with very different professional roles and responsibilities, it's important to really understand who you are and the context within which you're operating. As you can already see, process is going to look very different from one person to the next. Tom Brady's processes as a football champion will be quite different from a tennis star like Serena Williams's, and different again from what Thomas, our marketing leader, needs to do to scale commensurately with his organization. Thus, it's important that processes are grounded in who you are and the role you are in now. Just as we saw with the first P, purpose, process can and will change according to context and circumstance.

Here are the types of questions I ask every client at the start of our coaching engagement. As you read along, consider them for yourself and jot down your answers.

Understand Your Baseline Context

What is the purpose, vision, or overall goals you are working toward? What processes or structures do you currently have in place that support meeting those?

Determine Your Personal Preferences

How do you feel about process and structure? Do you naturally gravitate toward structure, or do you find yourself resisting it? The reality is that some of us love routine while for others, like Thomas, too much routine can feel like a cage. Some of us do best when every fifteen-minute block in the Outlook calendar is accounted for; others flourish with more flexibility in the schedule. The key is to know where you fall on the structured-unstructured continuum and implement processes that free up mindshare and time without feeling like unnecessary bureaucracy is bogging you down.

We want to hit that happy medium of providing sufficient structure for ourselves without feeling constricted. Once again, it's vitally important to self-spectate and know yourself (and for managers to know their direct reports), because a mismatch between your placement on the structured-unstructured continuum and your role can lead to stifled creativity and innovation, ineffectiveness, and eventually employee burnout. Creative and "free-thinker" types can feel hamstrung by too much routine and ritual, while those who need firm plans and boundaries in place can become overwhelmed with too much unstructured time. We want to reap the benefits of process and structure without sliding into any downsides.

What is your natural energy rhythm and pace? Do you prefer to operate in a "steady-as-she-goes" way, or are you naturally a "burst tasker"? A key part of sustaining Leader A mode is realizing that energy flows differently within each person, and it's important to come to understand how to best care for yours. Some of us operate at our best when we're paced in a smooth and steady way. Think of a light. "Steady as she goes" prefers to hold the light at a continuous level of brightness—not too bright, not too dim—at any given time. If this is you, then it's important that you have processes that ensure your best chance of having roughly the same workload and workflow each day.

Further, because we'll all have occasional crunch times, your processes should build in adequate time for a recharge after a period of sprinting. Ideally, you'll want some downtime *before* a period of intense work as well. Without processes that protect your energy flow, the steady-as-she-goes leader runs the risk of fueling the burst of energy required for a sprint with anxiety and adrenaline, and then feeling exhausted and burned out once the task is done. Too many of these peaks and valleys for the steady-as-she-goes leader can even undermine a career.

At the other end of the continuum are those professionals who are natural burst taskers. They derive energy and juice from the quick hits and hard drives required to push a deliverable over the finish line. They prefer to go all in, with all they've got. And when they are on, they are *on*—the light is at 110 percent brightness. Then likewise when they're off, they're fully off. Burst taskers love the thrill of the deal, and once they've sealed the deal, they need to fully recharge (we'll look at ways to do that later in the chapter). They excel in a pinch and thrive in any situation that requires quick deliverables, fast results, or even a steep learning curve that would leave others dismayed.

But burst taskers can often have trouble with tasks or initiatives that require a longer arc of time to complete. Some of these leaders describe almost having "leadership ADD" and are drained by processes or activities that require them to operate in sustain mode. Burst taskers thus need processes that keep the pace quick, the novelty high, and the deadlines coming.

When is your energy highest throughout the day? We all have different internal clocks, known as circadian rhythms, that govern our sleep cycles as well as our energy levels throughout the day.

Some people are natural early risers and never need an alarm clock, while others will hit the snooze button three times and don't really come to life until midmorning. It's important to be familiar with your own individual pattern, as your circadian rhythms can determine your ideal work schedule. For most people, research shows that peaks in alertness occur twice during the day: within an hour or so of noon, and again within an hour or so of 6 p.m. Thus, you should schedule your most important tasks within those windows of peak alertness, and your least important tasks during the hours when alertness is typically lowest: very early morning, around 3 p.m., and late at night.[2]

Sleep researcher and management professor Christopher M. Barnes points out that often, we get this exactly wrong. Many employees find themselves working through the morning just to respond to email, which eats up their valuable first peak of alertness. It's only after the postlunchtime slump that they're free to turn to tasks that require more cognitive energy and higher processing—and often, employees are expected to meet an end-of-day deadline, which means their best efforts are expected at the time of their lowest energy. The workday ends as the next peak of energy begins, and in the worst-case scenario, employees work into the night, "well into the worst circadian dip of the entire cycle."[3]

What's the best-case scenario? Match your work schedule with your chronotype, or your own natural circadian rhythm. If you are a lark, or a natural early riser, be aware of the impact of working late. Conversely, if you are an owl, the lark's late-night counterpart, do what you can to minimize working early shifts. These "chronotype mismatches" too easily make for unhappy, ineffective workers.[4]

Honor Your Preferences and Energy Flows

Process is one of the best ways we can honor our natural rhythms and practice good self-care. The goal is to build processes that suit your personality, your role, and your work environment. Often at the first sign of being pulled into a pitfall, the best response is to check and see if you've gotten lax with process. It could be that your processes no longer fit your current role, or perhaps you'll discover a mismatch somewhere between your processes and your natural proclivities.

After answering the process questions, Deepti, a systems engineer at a tech firm, had a big aha moment. She realized she was a steady-as-she-goes person but often procrastinated and ended up defaulting to burst-tasking to get things over the finish line. The process questions helped her understand why she got sick so often after major bursts and deliverables, and why she was feeling so drained generally. She realized that she wasn't honoring the pacing and restoration that her body and energy system needed. In terms of her specific daily processes, she realized that she tended to do emails in the morning, burning up her highest and most alert hours in the day, and saved high-productivity, intellectually demanding work for night.

Now aware of where her processes weren't serving her, Deepti and I made changes based on what would honor both her cognitive processes and energy flows, while also making sure that the processes enhanced her overall presence and effectiveness. For Deepti, we found that blocking time for restoration after travel days or after major events was critical to maintaining her performance and reducing her sick days. We also switched when she answered email and when she engaged in work that demanded her focus and attention so that she was doing harder work at times when she had more energy.

Thomas found the opposite after answering the process questions. Thomas most loved when he was at the start of a new product development cycle, when things were new and exciting. When the company was smaller, he was motivated by all the action happening in a growing company. He realized that part of what was draining his energy was that the company was now much bigger and more of his role was shifting toward helping his team to sustain and embed some of the new changes and processes the organization had recently implemented. He was spending more and more time inside the company rather than being out in the market. He wasn't tired because of the hours he was putting in; he was feeling drained because of the type of activities he was engaged in.

For burst taskers like Thomas, I often recommend two tactics. One is to see the benefits that greater predictability can bring.

When you're working toward more steady-as-she-goes goals, you, your team, and your loved ones at home can count on knowing when you'll deliver and when you'll be available. As one colleague described, it's like a squirrel storing acorns for the winter. The second tactic is to set up a series of interim deadlines and milestones so as to model the sprints and short bursts. This way you're making steady progress *and* working within the framework that comes most naturally and gives you the most energy.

For either type, if you find you're in a role that is completely opposite to what your natural pacing is, go back to the section in chapter 2 on evaluating whether it might be time for a role change. While Thomas hadn't yet reached this point, he acknowledged that at some point the company could hit a size where his work wouldn't excite him, and he'd need to keep an eye on that. Knowing what size and stage of company you prefer to work and lead in can make a big difference to your longer-term career satisfaction. If you are someone who likes to drive a speedboat, be mindful of taking on jobs in organizations that operate at a pace more like that of a cruise ship.

EXERCISE

Working with Your Natural Energy Flow

1. As you think about your own preferred pace, are you more of a burst tasker or steady-as-she-goes leader?

2. How does that line up with the current activities in your role today?

3. What changes, if any, can you make to better align your activities to your energy?

As you head into the next sections of this chapter, which provide advice on developing your own systems and processes, understand that these ideas are not exhaustive, nor do they fit everyone. I've included the ideas and strategies that have consistently yielded the best results for those I've worked with. As you go through them, make a check mark by ones you potentially would like to add to your personal operating system.

Preserve Your Time for What Matters Most

In Thomas's case, a lack of personal process and structure was starting to impede his sense of freedom. The fact is, if we don't proactively protect our time, it will get eaten away. The goal now for Thomas was to implement enough process that he could take back a feeling of control and enact a greater sense of choice and agency, which he felt he was losing.

Here are some of my favorite tips for ensuring we're directing our time toward what matters most.

Use Color Coding

Using color coding to track the activities in your calendar is one of the easiest process upgrades you can make. It's also one of the first I implement with clients to make sure they are focused on the upper-right quadrant (Quadrant I) of the purpose quadrants (in chapter 2).

This is a system I use in my own calendar too. What I like about it is the colors give me an easy way to check that my time is being spent on what matters most—and to readjust if it doesn't. As I enter activities, tasks, and meetings into my calendar, I code them in the following way:

- BLUE FOR QUADRANT I: These are QI activities, tasks, and meetings that are both "high contribution" and "high passion." These are the "sweet-spot" activities, in that they are aligned to my current purpose and include things like writing and speaking events.

- PURPLE FOR QUADRANT II: These are the activities that provide high contribution but are of lower passion for me.

While I know there are parts of my role as a firm leader that are important to engage in, my team and especially my assistant know that if there is too much purple on the calendar, watch out—they'll likely get the worst from me. I've used these purple spots in my calendar to help me make important hiring, delegating, and outsourcing decisions.

- YELLOW FOR QUADRANT III: I still enjoy these parts of my work, but I know they're no longer my highest and best use. I do keep some yellow for my own juice, but I know it's important that I offer some of these opportunities to other members of my team so they grow and develop as well.

- NO COLOR FOR QUADRANT IV: These are activities that don't move the needle and are low passion and low contribution. I try to keep these off my calendar, but when they do appear, I know it's time to think about delegating, hiring, or outsourcing.

An example of what my color coding for work looks like is shown in figure 3-1.

FIGURE 3-1

Color code what matters most into your calendar

		Contribution	
		Low/unclear	High
Passion	High	Quadrant III: Elevate (yourself or the idea) COLOR CODE YELLOW	Quadrant I: Prioritize (the sweet spot) COLOR CODE BLUE
	Low	Quadrant IV: Eliminate (or delegate, outsource, or hire) NO COLOR	Quadrant II: Tolerate (or delegate, outsource, or hire) COLOR CODE PURPLE

Color coding has made a big difference in my personal life as well. Here's what my personal color coding looks like:

- RED FOR SELF-CARE: This one is actually the most difficult for me; I find that giving myself permission for self-care is rarely at the top of the priority list. This is probably the spottiest color on the calendar and one I'm trying to increase.

- ORANGE FOR TIME I SPEND WITH MY SON, JORDAN: This includes things like school drop-offs and pickups when I can, attending karate practices, and making it to volleyball. I value this time immensely and try to make sure there's enough orange in my calendar.

- LIGHT GREEN FOR TIME I SPEND WITH FRIENDS AND EXTENDED FAMILY: When I see light green begin to disappear from my calendar, it's a cue to get out of "work mode" and ensure that I'm keeping an eye on other parts of my life and attending to important relationships.

The reason this system works so well is that it allows me to quickly take a longer view on how I spend my time and identify emerging patterns. There are no statistics to collect or analyses to run (which you may not have time to conduct anyway). All you have to do is take a look at your calendar and see what the colors tell you.

It can be especially helpful when transitioning into a larger role to use color coding to ensure that you are making time for the new responsibilities you're taking on. In consulting firms, law firms, and private equity firms, for example, at more senior levels you must be able to shift from more client-delivery or execution roles to also building in time for business development, sourcing, and firm-management activities, all of which can be color-coded into your calendar.

A longer view can help to confirm when you have given focus to something important, provide a red flag when something is not getting attended to for an extended period, or signal it's time to pivot when a major deliverable is completed. The colors serve as a cue to adapt as needed. Ultimately, you have to recognize that the colors will never be perfectly balanced or evenly spaced. They express the many different parts of yourself and what's most important to you now. They give you a way of making sure no one part of you or your role is getting shortchanged.

Set Power Hours

Another process upgrade to consider is instituting power hours into your schedule. These are spans of time that you set aside to focus on important tasks. This can be especially important for those who work for themselves or work from home, where building structure and discipline into the day helps to ensure that you use your time wisely, or for those who work in an office and are in meetings all day. Here's how to implement power hours into your schedule:

- Preset one to three power-hour blocks on your weekly calendar.

- An optimal power-hour block is about ninety minutes. (Research has shown that the ideal brain oscillation, or the time it takes to spend and recover mental energy, is ninety minutes.[5])

- Choose the block based on the time of day when you have the greatest clarity of mind and are generally most productive.

Granted, it's likely that some of these blocks will get scheduled over. But you have a far better shot at keeping them or at least some portion of them by putting them in your calendar. Three power hours a week seems to be the maximum I've observed busy leaders can preserve.

Because Thomas was more regularly presenting to the executive team on marketing analytics and data, he found that having power hours was critical to prepare for these high-stakes meetings. These meetings required Thomas to pivot from his more informal, shoot-from-the-hip approach, which worked great with customers and his team, to more structured time and prep that was more effective in the boardroom.

Leaders are often amazed how much they can get done during their power hours. Many people find they're more productive during these preset, small windows of time rather than longer, unstructured spans because power hours have a way of sharpening our focus and giving us a quick deadline to meet.

Determine Your Home Zones and Time Zones

Many leaders share that despite the tremendous success they experience at work and in their organizations, they still experience a fair amount of guilt and stress when trying to be present and engaged when they're at home with their loved ones or with friends. Work seems to creep into every part of their lives.

One leader named Joe was really struggling with this. Successful and effective in his business, Joe's marriage and family were getting shortchanged. Joe shared that his wife had reached her limit with him being distracted and preoccupied at home. He described feeling the constant urge to pick up his cell phone or laptop when he was with his family in the evenings and on the weekends.

Knowing that a great many of us, like Joe, must spend at least some hours working at home, my suggestion is to establish some clear boundaries around both time and physical space. Think of your "time zones" like your power hours. Find blocks of productive work time that will work for both you and your family. For example, Joe came up with the following time zones on a Saturday so that family didn't leak into work and work didn't leak into family:

> 8:00ISH: Wake up at later time than the usual 5:30 a.m.; no electronics by bed

> 9:00–10:00: Have a nice breakfast with family, being fully present

> 10:00–NOON: After breakfast, get in some "power hours" to catch up on work in home office

> NOON ON: Be present, have fun with friends or family for the rest of the day

"Home zones," meanwhile, are the physical spaces in your house you will go to—such as your home office or den—to get a little extra work done or crank through those emails. Time zones and home zones can help you communicate your availability to others both at work and on the home front, or set their expectations about your level of presence and engagement.

If you leave your electronics only in your designated home zones, you physically have to walk a distance to get to them. This is important given the psychological pull these devices have on us. Recent research indicates that merely having a smartphone nearby—even if you're not actively using it and even if it's powered off—impairs cognitive capacity. Why? The research suggests that our smartphones exert a *constant* pull on our attention. In effect, even if we think we're fully engaged in a task, part of us is always on alert for that next text message or email. In one study, the subjects who performed best on tests of cognitive capacity were the ones who put their phones in another room. The subjects who kept their phones beside them on their desks had the lowest scores—even though their phones were facedown and powered off.[6] By leaving electronics in a home zone, you are less likely to be tempted by them, and you're far more likely to be fully engaged in whatever you're doing at the moment. If you do succumb to temptation, you at least slow down your reaction time, and with enough practice, you can break the habit of reflexively reaching for a device.

Cal Henderson, the CEO of Slack, has a carefully routinized schedule and designated zones that allow him to maintain high productivity and enjoy uninterrupted time with family. In addition to preset blocks of time for work, exercise, and even a weekly date night with his wife, he shared in a recent interview with *Inc.* that he gets "two to three hours a day with [his] 2-year-old son during the week (an hour in the morning and an hour or more in the evening)," making it a point not to work during those hours. Henderson also includes walking to and from work and doing walking one-on-ones in order to get in time for exercise, setting a ten-minute countdown so meetings don't go overtime, and reserving a half hour in the midafternoon for brainstorming.[7]

FROM POST-ITS TO TECHNOLOGY APPS— KEEPING IT ALL ORGANIZED

Keeping your eye on what matters most also means you have a way to track and organize all the thousands of to-do items across your work and home life. These processes can make a significant impact on your mental clarity and level of anxiety. The litany of things we must remember across everything we lead and manage can be overwhelming. New follow-up items and to-dos seem to emerge out of every new meeting. Despite how good some of us think we are at multitasking, neuroscience research has shown that our brains can hold and process no more than two complex tasks at once—and even then, our brains "divide and conquer" by devoting one hemisphere to one task, the other hemisphere to another.[a] As with all the Ps, the key here is to continue to be true to who you are and to what feeds your energy and Leader A, even down to making choices between using something as old-school as Post-it notes all the way to lots of cutting-edge apps to help you protect your time, stay organized, and remain mentally clear.

- GOOD OL' PEN AND PAPER: Many of my clients find that they still value good ol' pen and paper for their processes. One leader, Joel, found that the single most critical process to his day was writing on a simple Post-it note the three most important things to get done that day, including both work and personal items. He said that as long as he hit those three items, he could let go of the guilt he was feeling for all that he did not get done and still preserve a sense of satisfaction from a job well done.

  Another leader, Ming, found she needed something that would not feel so uptight and rigid, yet still kept her from feeling like things were starting to fall through the cracks. After some experimentation, she decided to print out her Outlook calendar each day and carry it around in a plastic folder. During each meeting, as new items and follow-up tasks came up, she jotted a few notes to herself on the printout of the day's calendar. Then every Sunday, during her designated "time zone" and in her designated "home zone," she pulled out the plastic folder, which now housed five days' worth of notes, and looked back through and prioritized.

- **THE LATEST TECHNOLOGY:** Of course, on the other end of the spectrum, I know others who love tech and upgrade their processes with the latest tech available. Following are some of the applications I've observed clients use with success. The key is to shop around for what works best for you.

- **PROJECT MANAGEMENT TOOLS:** When you have many things to house, including task lists and documents, and want to share them with others, programs such as Asana and Basecamp can help to keep it all organized.

- **EMAIL MANAGEMENT PROGRAMS:** Managing email can be a full-time job if you aren't careful. Clients have shared that using a program like Boomerang can act like a snooze button, helping you to manage messages that you can't deal with today but that may need a response later.

- **CONTACT RELATIONSHIP MANAGEMENT TOOLS:** Especially for those who run small businesses or are independent contractors to businesses of all kinds, having a way to manage all your contacts and relationships is critical. You can prevent losing track of vital contacts especially in your business development or marketing efforts through programs such as Constant Contact, Mailchimp, Zoho CRM, and Freshsales.

- **CALENDAR SCHEDULING TOOLS:** If you work on your own or in an organization where you don't have an assistant, there are great tools such as Calendly and FreeBusy that can help with scheduling.

a. Gisela Telis, "Multitasking Splits the Brain," *Science*, April 15, 2010, http://www.sciencemag.org/news/2010/04/multitasking-splits-brain.

Employ Look-Aheads

Look-aheads help with planning and setting expectations with others and can be employed across many different time frames. An easy way to set these up is by time frame:

- ANNUALLY: Block vacation windows, school performances, conferences, or other important events for the year.

- QUARTERLY/MONTHLY: Look for travel, deadlines, or busy periods to plan for.

- WEEKLY/DAILY: Look for a meeting where a little extra prep could make a difference to the outcome.

Choosing the best time frame is really a function of your own work context. One leader shared how his organization operated on short cycle times. Weekly and monthly time frames didn't matter because things were always in flux. In his case, we added a short look-ahead to the start of each day to replace his habit of coming into the office and clearing email. Now, he scans for the upcoming meetings for the day and does some prep on the one or two that are especially important. Whatever your context and responsibilities, how you start your day can be critically important to how you feel the rest of the day, so block at least the first fifteen to thirty minutes for no meetings, and stay off email until you've identified your priorities for the day.

Another leader found that the look-ahead became critical for his family. Every Sunday morning at breakfast, the family all pulled out their laptops—his teenagers included—to do a quick scan of the week on who was doing what and who was going to be where, and to flag any important information for each other. It not only became a form of quality time together but kept all of them in greater sync with each other before heading into the week.

Make the Most of White Space

Sometimes a meeting is canceled or gets rescheduled, or perhaps you have an awkward thirty-minute gap between two important things.

You may have a train ride home that takes longer than expected. All too often we're paralyzed by the possibilities of what we could do with this "white space" on our daily calendars, expected or not, so we fritter these open windows away by looking at our phones. Then we kick ourselves later for not using the time well.

Believe it or not, the best way to make the most of white space is to decide in advance how you want to use that kind of time. One leader, Alex, described feeling especially frustrated by a long train ride home every evening after work. He found that he spent the entire sixty minutes standing and scrolling through articles on his phone. He was exasperated by how meaningless that time was.

I asked Alex to create two lists for himself: a "productive white-space list" and a "restorative white-space list." The intent of each is just what it sounds like: in productive white space, he'd use the time to complete necessary tasks. In restorative white space, he'd allow himself time to do nonwork things that would help him relax and recharge. Here's what his lists looked like:

TABLE 3-1

Example of white-space lists

Alex's productive white-space list	Alex's restorative white-space list
• Brainstorm on a passion project	• Close eyes, rest, and breathe
• Write emails or texts	• Listen to music, a book on tape, or a meditation app
• Make calls like setting up appointments	• Call a friend to check in and say hi

What you choose when white space emerges is ultimately a function of a few questions:

- How much time do I have?

- What is realistic to accomplish?

- What would be most satisfying at this time?

Having a list in advance brings ideas more readily to mind when those moments present themselves, and it reduces the chances that you'll let the time get away from you. After a few weeks of trying it out, listening to audiobooks became Alex's preferred white-space

FREE-THINKING TIME

Nature does not hurry, yet everything is accomplished.
—Lao Tzu

Everyone from the great ancient sages to contemporary neuroscientists and productivity experts tout the value of periodic unstructured time. Especially if you're in a creative field—or maybe you just need to think your way through a thorny problem at work—the mind needs time to recharge, roam, free-associate, and make unexpected connections. Some of our greatest thought leaders, from Einstein to Steve Jobs to Beethoven, were known to take long walks in order to generate ideas and problem-solve.

You can actually build this time into your personal operating system through either your power hours or use of white space to ensure having unstructured time. One of my colleagues, for example, blocks off Fridays from 2:00–3:00 p.m. as his power hour for free thinking. If the weather cooperates, he spends the hour outside strolling; if not, he closes his office door and, with pen and paper before him, doodles and jots down ideas as they come to him.

In a similar vein, Bill Gates is known for his "think weeks." Twice a year, he schedules a seven-day stretch of seclusion to ponder the future of technology. During this week he takes no calls and receives no visitors—including family and Microsoft staff—save for

activity. He's enjoying books he's always meant to read, and he found that recharging in this way allowed him to arrive home after a long day at work feeling more rested and far less frustrated. Feeling recharged, he was able to be fully present with his partner and that much more productive at work.

Use the Brush Your Teeth Practice

The short investments of time you make in power hours or during white spaces add up. I've come to think of this as the a caretaker who slips him two meals a day. Upon returning, he shares his ideas with the entire Microsoft empire.[a]

While most of us won't have the luxury of a week, the idea of giving ourselves some solo time to think, be more reflective, or connect the dots has great value. One leader I know takes a day or two a month off but doesn't go anywhere; this is her time to be on vacation from the outside world so she can get in some critical reflection, thinking, and restorative time. Others schedule this solo time at key milestones, such as when they need to write their annual self-evaluation, during winter holidays to step back and take stock of the year, or at the start of the new year to be more intentional about what's to come.

Even making sure you have an extra day to yourself at the end of vacation can make a difference to your presence and mental clarity. Rather than jamming it all into five days, for example, take four days for having fun and then a day of transition to get back into the flow. For that final transition day, pick your favorite process to signal to yourself that you're shifting gears. You'll get more from the vacation's restorative time this way.

a. Robert A. Guth, "In Secret Hideaway, Bill Gates Ponders Microsoft's Future," *Wall Street Journal*, March 28, 2005, https://www.wsj.com/articles/SB111196625 830690477.

brushing teeth practice. Brushing your teeth is an activity we do every day that takes just minutes but is vastly important and has a positive cumulative effect on our health. If you maintain small but steady progress on long-term projects or break down a task into short chunks of time, added up over the course of a week, month, or quarter, you've made progress and maybe even completed a project.

This practice was incredibly important for Deepti as it allowed her to keep a steady pace to match her natural rhythm and pacing. It helped her numerous times to get to the end zone on important

PROCESS UPGRADES FOR YOUR TEAM OR ORGANIZATION

Like Thomas, many leaders find when their organizations are going through periods of hypergrowth and transformation, they need to reboot not only their own personal operating system and processes but key team and organizational processes as well.

Following are three areas every leader should have an eye on regarding team or organization-wide process upgrades. As you think of key stakeholders you engage with, such as direct reports, teams, or the board, ask yourself if there is an opportunity to reboot:

- **THE CADENCE AND EFFECTIVENESS OF MEETINGS:** How often are you meeting with your teams as a collective group as well as for one-on-ones? For what the group needs to achieve, do you have the optimal cadence for recurring meetings? For example, after receiving critical funding from new investors, one executive team suddenly found themselves with a much more formal board. The CEO quickly put in place a new cadence in terms of the team coming together before the board meeting to ensure that they had pressure-tested the agenda and ideas and were heading in as a united front. Likewise, this CEO recognized the importance of what happened after board meetings as well, and instituted a process for how the team would debrief after each one.

  One of the books I recommend to all leaders trying to build great teams and processes is Patrick Lencioni's *The Advantage*.

large projects and presentations. By putting in thirty- to sixty-minute blocks, which was often all the time she could afford in a given day, she was more likely to get something done after a week than waiting for some imaginary eight-hour block to finish in one sitting.

A key chapter in that book is called "The Centrality of Great Meetings," and I highlight it here because so much of team and organizational life is lived in meetings. Much of having a Leader A or B day at work depends on how effective those meetings are.

- THE CADENCE AND EFFECTIVENESS OF COMMUNICATIONS: In addition to assessing their meetings, leaders like Thomas who find themselves in growing roles and organizations need to pause and give thought to their communications. How should he cascade important information—how often and through what vehicles? This review gave Thomas and me an opportunity to reoptimize and consider a greater visibility plan for him, including more informal "walk-arounds" of the office, more structured email updates, and a more defined flow for his all-hands meetings.

- DEFINING AND TRACKING MEASURES OF SUCCESS: Another key process to keep your eye on is measuring success. How do you know if you, your team, and your organization are focused on what matters most? What metrics are critical to the business? Which ones show how you are making a difference? Depending on your role, this could include how you build dashboards, scorecards, and objectives for your teams and organization.

Maintain Processes That Recharge and Restore Your Energy

While protecting your time for what matters most is critical, it's equally important to protect and restore your energy to feed Leader A.

While we've covered getting in some restoration when white space emerges, you can also intentionally build in processes and create cycles for when you can restore and recharge.

Scientific evidence supports the value of this cyclical form of operating for our mental and physical well-being, as well as for our productivity. Rather than trying to "tough it out" and power through the workday when we're physically or mentally depleted, research suggests that it's better to stop, fully recover, and try again. Why does this approach work better than trying to "grin and bear it"? Because of the fundamental biological concept called homeostasis, or the ability of the brain to continuously restore and sustain well-being. Neuroscientist Brent Furl coined the term *homeostatic value* to describe the value that certain practices and actions have for creating equilibrium, and thus well-being, in the body. When the body is out of alignment from overworking, we waste a great deal of mental and physical energy trying to return to balance before we can move forward.[8] It's therefore far better to give ourselves time to recover and then, refreshed, return to our work with the battery recharged. How widespread is the problem of overworked, exhausted, and unproductive workers? A recent study found that a lack of recovery—whether due to disrupted sleep or being in a state of continuous cognitive arousal by staring at our screens—is costing US companies $62 billion a year in lost productivity. When we're in a state of exhaustion, we simply don't have the cognitive or physical resources to perform at our best.[9]

Recharging can come in many forms. I often like to think of it on a continuum from more passive forms of restoration to more active ones, as figure 3-2 illustrates. I've noticed that many leaders gravitate only to the more active forms, so I encourage you to take more of a portfolio approach toward having a variety of ways to restore and recover.

Twenty years ago when I was a management consultant working one hundred hours a week, I suffered from chronic back and neck pain. It took a couple of years to fully recover, and though I did, I still struggle to give myself permission to restore my body and energy periodically. This experience, however, led me to insist on addressing self-care with every leader I work with. Following are

FIGURE 3-2

Forms of energy recharge

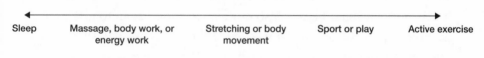

ideas I've experimented with myself and discussed with other colleagues and leaders who are in search of rituals that best support Leader A.

Employ the Midweek Gas Tank Fill-Up

On the left side of the continuum is good old-fashioned sleep. We all know that sleep is critical to our performance and productivity. In the book *The Sleep Revolution*, Arianna Huffington wrote, "We sacrifice sleep in the name of productivity, but ironically our loss of sleep, despite the extra hours we spend at work, adds up to 11 days of lost productivity per year per worker, or about $2,280."[10] Getting enough sleep—seven to eight hours a night is recommended—is critical, but I've seen friends and clients spend way too much time stressing about not getting as much sleep as they think they should.

Instead of trying to force yourself to get a solid eight every single night, develop a sleep ritual or process that is more realistic for you. For example, for one leader, Aton, sleep was a critical performance lever and directly impacted his ability, especially to speak and present articulately, concisely, and clearly. However, Aton was in a job that made getting eight hours of sleep a night unrealistic. We therefore had to figure out a process that fit his context and role but also ritualized his need for extra sleep. We came up with the "midweek gas tank fill-up" ritual. Sometime midweek, Aton would get one or two nights of great sleep—eight-plus hours, which was significantly more than the five to six hours he normally got. He was excited to find that the one or two nights more than filled up his gas tank and made a tremendous difference to his mental clarity and physical sense of well-being. Because his effectiveness and satisfaction were so directly tied to being more thoroughly rested, the midweek fill-up yielded a very high ROI. A naturally hard charger, Aton had never valued sleep or naps as much as he did a hard cardio workout. However, as he began to reap the benefits of greater sleep, he found that he was also more aware and began to give himself more permission on the weekends for an occasional afternoon nap as another way to restore his battery for the week to come.

Explore Passive Forms of Restoration

Like sleep, there are other ways to restore more passively—and help you rest more deeply. As a leader, you are often in action, leading, and driving things forward. Getting a massage can be a good way of allowing yourself to let go. For example, one colleague added to her processes an early morning massage two Saturdays a month. She said it was so nice to have a break from always being in charge—running the show at work and at home—and while she was on the table, she could allow "all the tension from work to seep into the ground."

According to the Mayo Clinic, massage can help reduce stress, anxiety, muscle tension and pain, headaches, digestive disorders, and insomnia. And as the benefits of massage have become more widely known, massage is no longer available only through luxury spas or upscale health clubs. It's now offered in businesses, clinics, hospitals, and even airports and malls, at much more affordable prices.[11]

There are alternative modalities that move beyond releasing muscle tension and also work with the energy fields around the body. Examples of this type of "bodywork" include acupuncture, Reiki, and cranial sacral therapy. While these forms aren't for everyone, practitioners say that improving the flow of energy around the body promotes relaxation, reduces pain, speeds healing, and reduces other symptoms of illness.[12]

Frankly, anything that takes you out of the driver's seat and gives you some personal attention—like getting a haircut or getting your nails done, for instance—can have a restorative benefit. But of course, take care that your self-care isn't another "should." You don't want it to be one more thing on the to-do list or another appointment that crowds your calendar. Instead, look at these practices as a way to give yourself some quiet time and allow someone else to give energy back to you.

Stretch (Anytime, Anywhere)

So much of our day is now spent sitting at our desks or on a plane, where key muscles tighten and contract. Additionally, our necks, shoulders, and arms become tight from so many hours spent hunched over a laptop. According to Harvard Medical School, we all need to stretch in order to protect our mobility and independence for the long term. Stretching keeps the muscles flexible, strong, and healthy, and we need that flexibility to maintain a range of motion in the joints.[13]

You can stretch anywhere and anytime—at your desk, in your office, or at night, right before bed. When creating processes or rituals, pick a cue to signal to yourself, *it's time*. Midday right before lunch is often a good time to get off your laptop and take a stretch.

I'm also a big fan of YouTube videos that you can use anywhere to get in a meaningful stretch. For example, check out "Fitness Blender: Upper Body Stretching Routine" or "Fitness Blender: Upper Body Active Stretch Workout—Arms, Shoulder, Chest, and Back Stretching Exercises." They're less than fifteen minutes each, and they fully stretch out the upper body after a long morning at the computer.

For those who are open to yoga, I also love Rodney Yee's videos on YouTube. Check out his chair series, which you can actually do at your desk: his "4-Minute Neck and Shoulders Stretch at Your Desk" and "Desk Yoga: Stress-Relieving Back Stretches to Do in Your Chair" are both under five minutes long.

Recharge through Sports and Exercise

In addition to the more gentle and passive forms of rest and restoration noted so far, we can also recharge ourselves through movement, sports, and exercise. The key is to find a sport, movement, or exercise you enjoy.

The best kind of exercise is whatever personally brings you into a state of flow and presence—a feeling of being more alive—and leaves you with a greater sense of freedom. As you get more on top of your calendar through color coding and many of the other tips in this chapter, the more you'll be able to create time for this much-needed form of energy recharge.

Thomas, our marketing leader and natural burst tasker, loved to mountain bike. Thomas shared how the thrill of being on his bike and out in nature always left him feeling free and more alive. To fit biking into his already busy schedule, Thomas did two things: he joined a local cycling club, and he color-coded into his calendar a monthly ride with them to protect this time and prioritize cycling. He couldn't make it to their weekly events, but he could fit in a monthly ride, and the accountability he got from putting it into his calendar and riding with his new peers helped keep him on track.

In addition to the obvious cardiovascular and musculoskeletal benefits that regular exercise brings, a host of new brain research confirms that exercise boosts mood, reduces anxiety, and even protects against cognitive decline and depression.[14] A recent article from *Fast Company* also offers some fascinating insight into what happens on a neurological level when we exercise—and gives busy leaders some heartening reassurance. It seems that when we start exercising, our brains recognize this as a moment of stress: your brain thinks you're either fighting an enemy or fleeing from it. The brain responds with a self-protective mechanism: it triggers the release of a protein called BDNF (brain-derived neurotrophic factor). BDNF helps to protect and repair memory neurons and also acts as a reset switch, which is why we often feel at ease and clearheaded after exercising. As for that fabled runner's high, or the euphoria associated with exercising, that's the result of another chemical the brain releases to fight stress. Endorphins can minimize the pain and discomfort associated with exercise and are responsible for that feeling of euphoria. So it's BDNF plus endorphins that make exercise feel so good.[15]

But there's more good news. *New York Times* best-selling author Gretchen Reynolds has written a book on the mental and physical benefits of exercise called *The First 20 Minutes*. According to Reynolds, we don't need to become professional athletes in order to get the best benefits for health or happiness. On the contrary, smaller amounts of exercise are sufficient to boost happiness and productivity, and in fact, it's in the first twenty minutes of exercise that the major health benefits such as prolonged life and reduced disease risk arrive.[16] So when you're in a time crunch, you can cut yourself some slack, knowing that if you can get in twenty focused minutes, you're still doing your body and your mind a favor.

Putting It All Together: Rituals for the Road

For many leaders, work travel accounts for a disproportionate amount of their time and energy. Creating rituals and processes to optimize your time on the road can make all the difference in keeping your energy sustained, as opposed to coming back feeling absolutely drained and unhealthy. There is a clear association between frequent business travel and a higher risk of chronic disease. A recent study examining health data from thousands of US employees produced some sobering findings. Compared to those who spent one to six nights a month away for business travel, those who spent fourteen or more nights away per month had significantly higher body mass index scores and were significantly more likely to report poor self-rated health; clinical symptoms of anxiety, depression, and alcohol dependence; no physical activity or exercise; smoking; and trouble sleeping. For those who traveled twenty-one or more nights per month, the odds of being obese were a staggering 92 percent higher compared to those who traveled only one to six nights per month. This "road-warrior" group also had higher blood pressure and lower HDL cholesterol (the so-called good cholesterol).[17] No matter how much you travel, time away comes with its own set of stresses and takes you out of your normal routine and processes, making it more difficult to exercise, eat healthfully, and get enough sleep. Here's how to keep feeding Leader A while you're on the road.

Be Judicious about Networking Time

Work travel often involves dinners and late nights. Employ a look-ahead ritual and take special note of the evenings where calling it a day earlier (perhaps you have an early morning flight the next day) or respectfully declining an invitation would be best. One of my colleagues who is also an author and speaks at special events shared with me how she became much more judicious about accepting client dinner invitations. Going out the evening before she was to serve as a speaker was negatively impacting her ability to deliver the next day. She noticed the conditions that led to her most successful events and found that the common denominator was a good night's rest and preparation. As a result, she let her clients know in advance she wouldn't be joining them the night before so she could deliver the highest level of quality. Instead, she stayed for any social events that followed her presentation.

Stay Productive on the Flight Out, Restorative on the Flight In

The great news is travel also inherently offers blocks of power hours. One leader who traveled almost two-thirds of the year became more intentional with his flight time. He decided that if it was going to be such a big part of his job, it was worth reoptimizing how he spent his energy on the road—or in the air. After some experimentation he came up with two rules of thumb. On the way out, he used the flight as productive white space, reviewing important documents, engaging in strategic reflection, or moving the needle on a top-priority item. After a long day of meetings and on his return flights home, he gave himself permission to relax. He used this flight time as restorative white space by listening to music, napping, or reading a book. This leader came up with a great reminder phrase for himself—*productive on the flight out, restore and relax on the flight in.*

If you're crunched for time, tighten this up and do it for takeoff and landing when you can't have a computer up. For example, Alexis Ohanian, the head of Reddit, said that he "read[s] a book during takeoff and landing periods, but as soon as that bell dings, the laptop is out and I'm online."[18]

Keep the Blood Circulating

A frustration I often hear is how work travel gets in the way of physical exercise. Let go of the expectation that your workout has to be perfect or can only be counted as exercise if you are on a treadmill or favorite running trail. And again, white spaces can come to the rescue. Look at all the places where you have white space when waiting to board a flight. During these windows, there usually isn't enough time to pull up the laptop and get anything meaningful accomplished, so too often, we end up on phones, mindlessly scrolling until the boarding agent calls our boarding group number. Next time, get in your movement and exercise. Bring a change of travel clothes so that after a long day of meetings you're in casual wear and walking shoes. Walk up and down the hallway of the airport and watch your Fitbit steps crank up. This is a great way to get some blood and oxygen circulating in the body before sitting on a long flight. You can do the same thing on the flight itself. Get up every hour to walk, move your body, stretch or shake out your legs, or circle your ankles to keep the circulation going.

Find Which Processes Work for You

If you naturally resist process and structure like Thomas, there is a good chance that you may feel overwhelmed with all this talk of process, and are wondering where and how to begin.

First, remember that process is unique to each person, and the key is finding what works for *you*. So rather than burdening yourself with another "should," reframe process as a commitment to yourself and to the purpose and vision you hope to achieve. Rather than a cage or a constraint, process is meant to be a support, and it can even be a means to greater liberation. With the right processes in place, we're less susceptible to pendulum swings between excessive spontaneity and rigid adherence to a schedule. We also become less dependent on moods or feeling states to drive our behaviors and actions, and instead have clearer, intentional choice and agency in how we choose to spend our time and energy. In short, our highest and best self is protected by our processes.

The second thing to remember is that process is one of our best ways of getting back on track quickly. What most of my clients have found is that there are one or two processes that play the biggest role in staying in Leader A mode and becoming much less susceptible to Leader B days. Take, for example, Joel, who had his Post-it note for his top three things. He found that this simple ritual could make for a really effective, present, and satisfying day. The great news was that whenever he started to feel overwhelmed or "off," he realized that all he had to do was reinstate the ritual— and he was back on track again. For Aton, the midweek gas tank fill-up was the process that most impacted his effectiveness and performance. Deepti found that the brushing her teeth practice was the best way to feed Leader A, and Thomas learned that keeping some semblance of power hours, even if abbreviated to a thirty-minute window, could make or break how he felt about a given day.

Give yourself some time to experiment, and then narrow the processes down to one or two that you must have, and see the rest as icing on the cake. One client said his top two processes reminded him of a hammock: with these routines in place, he could be at ease, knowing not only *what* was ahead, but *how* he was going to tackle the many tasks of the day. When you have a process that works, you make your best practices not a flash in the pan, but a daily habit you can rely on.

What to Remember:

➤ Being committed to process, structure, and rituals can enhance performance, save time, help you restore, and provide guardrails in a world where there is always more to do than hours to do it in. The second P, process, is like keeping a personal operating system up to date. Much like our laptops and smartphones, our processes are often due for a periodic upgrade.

➤ Process looks very different from one person to the next. It's important to create processes grounded in who you are and the role you are in now. Consider your relationship to process and structure and whether you are someone who naturally gravitates to it or resists it. You will want to have enough process to derive its benefits without letting it tip into unnecessary bureaucracy. Additionally, you should consider your natural energy flows and pacing—burst tasker or steady as she goes—and try to match activities to your chronotype and circadian rhythms as well.

➤ If you don't proactively protect your time, it will get eaten away. Let process help you take back a feeling of control and enact a greater sense of choice and agency. You can do this by looking back at your passion-contribution matrix from chapter 2 on purpose and set up your calendar to protect your highest and best activities—including color coding, power hours, look-aheads, time zones, and home zones.

➤ Research has validated the importance of restoration and recovery to our performance. Having a portfolio of processes—from more passive forms to more active ones—to restore and recharge your energy is important. Set up rituals that give you a better shot of getting rest and sleep, that relieve tension, or that help you experience a greater sense of freedom so you can keep the battery recharged.

➤ Many of the concepts in this chapter can be helpful for setting up rituals for the road. Limit your networking time, especially on evenings when getting to bed early is critical to your effectiveness the next day. Set up processes to maximize the flight out and the flight home, and still keep your blood circulating in airports and on planes, so you have a better shot at getting home feeling less drained.

The Power of People

Raise Your Game, Raise the Game of Others

Rajiv had just come from a one-on-one meeting with his boss, where he learned he'd been promoted to EVP of operations. The plan was to merge two functional areas of the organization, which would substantially increase the number of Rajiv's direct reports, including a group whose responsibilities weren't in his current realm of expertise. Rajiv had been working toward an executive-level role for years, and he and I had both assumed that when this day arrived, it would be one of celebration. But rather than being excited and happy, the first thought that popped into Rajiv's head was, how am I going to be able to do all of this?

Rajiv was a talented and self-aware leader. He excelled at operations, and although he was approachable and genuinely cared about his colleagues, he knew his Achilles heel was his hesitation when it came to people. Relative to his peers, Rajiv was slower to make moves or give feedback when team members were lower performing. He was also hesitant to delegate and always got a little more involved than he needed to be. In short, he was a leader who consistently fell into the I'll Just Do It Myself Pitfall—and he knew it.

Now with this new, elevated role, Rajiv knew he could no longer do things the way he had been. He'd have to learn to play at a higher level to avoid getting trapped in the weeds. And with the new responsibility of overseeing a group that worked in an area he did not know, he'd have to quickly become comfortable with not being the expert and rely more on asking others for support, which did not come naturally to him.

The Impact of People on Leader A and Leader B

My work with Rajiv and other leaders assuming larger roles or taking on exciting new challenges has shown me the importance of the third P, people, in supporting our effectiveness, presence, and satisfaction over time.

People—and here we're talking not just about your direct reports or team, but your entire network of support—can bring the capacity, energy, and support needed to meet a deadline, realize a big goal, or build a company with great success and scale. People are a direct contributing factor to our Leader A days when we feel like we're working toward a shared vision, or when the people we count on are present. On the flip side, people can be a contributing factor to Leader B days, especially when a key role on our team is vacant or when we feel drained by our interactions with others. The third P—people—impacts both our capacity and bandwidth as a leader as well as our capacity for how much we can hold and handle.

For this third P, it's critical to bring a Leader A mindset, which allows us to get comfortable with the idea of depending on others and considering how everyone can rise together. This requires that we are willing to let go, be vulnerable, ask for help, not have all the answers, see the unique value and contributions our colleagues bring, and not jump in each time anxiety or control gets the better of us. In fact, as one CEO said to me, "The goal is to make yourself not necessary." This doesn't mean you're stepping back—it means you're stepping *up* as a leader, which requires a greater focus on your team and their long-term success. At the same time, we must be able to maintain healthy boundaries and rules of engagement so that people do not drain us of energy, recognizing what's not ours to own, tactically or emotionally. When you're in a Leader A mindset, you care for yourself *and* for others. As Bill Gates said back in 2008 at the World Economic Forum's meeting in Davos, "There are two great forces of human nature—self-interest and caring for others."[1]

In this chapter, we will look at the third P of people through two different vantage points. The first is through the lens of the interdependence required to raise your game and raise the game of others. We'll start by examining the current strength of your team and then I'll show you how to optimize what I call the *leverage + empower + inspire equation*. We'll then take a deeper and more personal look at your current strategic network of support and see if you have the right people in place—and if you find that you don't, I'll offer some tips on how to find them. Next we'll look at the emotional autonomy and independence we must have to ensure that we're caring for ourselves. We'll end the chapter by examining the health of our boundaries and rules of engagement with others.

Examine the Strength of Your Team

Think about a team you work with today. It may be a traditional "top-down" structure wherein you have a direct line of authority over your team members (affectionately called "the lieutenant table" by some of the leaders I work with), or it may be a project team where there is a "dotted" line and you have more of an indirect influence over the team members.

The first step is to take a good hard look at your team today. No one's starting point is the same, but there are three important questions to ask yourself:

- What is the current strength of this team—do I have the right people on the bus?

- What changes to people or team structure will I need to make?

- What am I doing toward succession planning to build bench strength for the future?

Let's look at each of these in turn.

What is the current strength of this team—do I have the right people on the bus?

Consider the vision and goals you are working toward and whether the folks on your team have the capabilities needed. This can be very difficult for some leaders, especially if you've worked with members of your team for a long time and they're no longer the best fit for the job. Such was the case for Rajiv, for whom taking an objective look at his team created tension and angst. He was very comfortable with the folks he'd worked with for years—there were long-standing relationships and loyalties in place. However, as he and I discussed which 20 percent of the job was creating 80 percent of the energy drain he was feeling, he realized that a key direct report wasn't meeting the mark in their growing business. Rajiv had been picking up the slack for this person, falling into *two* pitfalls: I'll Just Do More and I'll Just Do It Myself. Covering for this underperforming employee meant Rajiv was having more Leader B than Leader A days. And in his new, larger role, he simply wasn't going to be able to compensate for his colleague.

What changes to people or team structure will I need to make?

You might find in looking at the team more closely that the fundamental team design and structure are off. Perhaps people need to be layered differently or reorganized. Or, like Rajiv, perhaps you realize there are team members who don't have the capabilities or aren't performing at a level the organization now needs.

In these cases, remember it's not fair to anyone to let a person languish in a role that is no longer suited for them. Jeff Weiner, CEO of LinkedIn, really shifted my view of this when I heard him speak about compassionate leadership. "The most important lesson I've learned in the role of CEO," he said, "is to not leave the pitcher in the game too long. . . . The least compassionate thing you can do when someone is not equipped to be doing what they're doing is to leave them in that role."[2] When you're the team leader, it's your job to be that coach walking out to the pitcher's mound and make the right call for the business and the person—even when it's a very difficult decision. When you're in a challenging situation like this one, ask yourself these questions:

- Is it time to have a difficult performance discussion?

- Is it time to invest in a development plan or coaching for this person?

- Is it time to let the person go?

Leadership does require that we sometimes give tough performance reviews, help a low performer get back on track, or occasionally, let someone go. With compassionate leadership and Weiner's counsel in mind, remember to make the tough "what" decisions and preserve your integrity and the other person's dignity in "how" you execute those decisions. When I ask leaders to reflect on the one thing they would have done differently from the previous year, the answer I most often hear is they wished they'd made a tough people decision sooner or faster—they wished they'd trusted their instincts that someone was wrong for the job or just not going to get there rather than letting it drag out.

What am I doing toward succession planning?

For some leaders the idea of succession planning may feel uncomfortable. Especially if, like Rajiv, you're just starting a new role and are motivated to add more value, you may be wondering why on earth I'm advising you to contemplate who is going to take on your position one day. But in order to keep growing and evolving your own purpose (chapter 2), you must have people who can eventually step into your shoes so that you and your organization are able to tackle future opportunities. You ultimately want to set in place a virtuous cycle so as you continue to grow and free yourself to take on new things → you are helping your people free up and take on news things → and then they can help others grow and take on new things. Many leaders underestimate how far in advance they need to start looking at this and don't always get it right.

Optimize the "Leverage + Empower + Inspire" Equation

Raising your game while raising the game of others also means that you continually look at what I call the leverage + empower + inspire equation. This is a critical equation to keep your eye on as you continue to grow as a leader, especially at key junctures such as when you shift from being a "leader of tasks" to a "leader of a team" to a "leader of leaders." At each of these junctures, you must redefine all three parts of the equation, which serve a different function but together form a powerful synergy.

Leverage: Get Clear on Who Owns What. The leverage part of the equation is about increasing your bandwidth and capacity. It requires that you rethink your level of involvement and ensure that everyone on the team is truly playing to their highest and best in their respective roles. You simply cannot be involved in all that you were in a previous role or when your organization was smaller. Ideally, you are providing your boss leverage, your team is providing you leverage, their teams are providing them leverage, and so on.

One tool that can be especially helpful here is the Who Owns What table. It's built on the same concepts of passion and contribution from chapter 2 on purpose.

- Think about your own role today and consider for column one the strategic initiatives you are responsible for as well as the normal duties that come with any job.

- Then, in columns two and three, bring over the information from chapter 2 about your purpose:

  - In column two, for each initiative or duty, what is your highest contribution?

TABLE 4-1

The Who Owns What table

	Your role/ function	What part of this is your highest contribution?	What part of this are you most passionate about?	What part of this can you get more leverage?	Who is the best person(s) to do that?
Key initiatives					
Normal responsibilities					

- In column three, for each initiative or duty, what is your highest passion?

- Now for column four, consider within a given initiative or duty where you could get more leverage, and finally, in column five, who might be the best person to do that.

The most optimal situation is that someone else's Quadrant I (their highest contribution and passion) is now your Quadrant IV (your lower contribution and passion). That is the ultimate win-win.

This is a great exercise to do at the start of each fiscal year. For example, last January I spent a half day with a leader working through the Who Owns What table against his team's functional plan. By the end of the exercise, for almost every major initiative or duty he was responsible for, we had identified the places where he could gain additional support from others to accomplish the functions' objectives. Imagine the relief and encouragement he felt once he'd identified the tasks that would allow his team to develop *and* buy himself more bandwidth and time.

Increasing leverage for yourself and your team isn't easy. It means getting more comfortable with being able to let go of things you used to do—in some cases, even things you really enjoy doing or you are good at or faster at than others—but may no longer be your highest and best use and could provide someone else on your team the opportunity to grow.

And be careful of going too far. If your sole intention is leverage, you run the risk of others feeling used or taken for granted. If you treat others simply as an extra set of hands for your sole benefit, you end up siphoning off the parts of the job you don't want to do while taking credit, or enjoying the high-visibility parts of the job alone.

The last watch-out? Some leaders may be good at leveraging, but when it's done without sharing context or without transparent decision making, or done without thinking of the other person's development, there is lost opportunity to help build the capability and business judgment of others. Therefore, leverage must come with the second dimension of our leverage + empower + inspire equation, empower.

Empower: Help Yourself and Others Spread Their Wings. The empower part of the leverage + empower + inspire equation focuses on building team capability and motivation. It requires that we think about how to offer freedom, autonomy, and authenticity to those we work with while setting them up for success as we offer more rope and opportunity. This requires looking at empowerment from two different perspectives. The first is from your own perspective, and the second is from the perspective of the team member you're trying to empower.

One of my favorite tools is the classic "T-shaped management" tool, which we can adapt for empowerment. In the original, the concept illustrated the dual responsibility of the executive who shares knowledge freely across the organization (the horizontal axis), while remaining committed to business performance (the vertical axis).[3] I've reframed the image in the following way:

As you look at empowerment from your own perspective and consider what you will let go of and when you will let it go, you can ask yourself the following questions:

- As I look across my span of control (along the horizontal line of the T), what is the full breadth of what's in my scope?

- Across that horizontal, where are the places I need to make vertical dives in?

FIGURE 4-1

T-shaped management tool adapted for empowering others

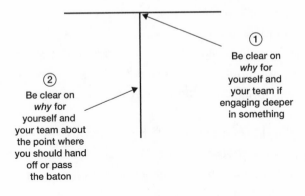

- When I start to make that vertical dive, what do I need to communicate to my team or direct report about WHY I'm getting involved?

- And, at what point along the vertical dive is it best I remove myself and pass the baton to someone else?

The other perspective you must take as a leader is putting yourself in the shoes of the team member you are trying to empower. The irony is that the best empowerment comes with being clear on the boundaries within which your team member or direct report has freedom to act. As you prepare to empower your team more, you can ask yourself the following questions:

- How will this opportunity help to grow this person's knowledge of the business, decision making/judgment, or visibility?

- What are the big risks to mitigate? Which ones are part of the learning experience?

- What context, information, or background can I offer?

- What are the expectations or definitions of success they should be aware of?

- What are the decision-making rights here?

THE SPECIAL RELATIONSHIP AND SUPPORT OF AN EA

Not all leaders have executive assistants, and I understand that for many organizations, this additional support is simply not possible. But for those who do or for professionals who are considering enlisting the help of an EA, the support can be invaluable.

In my coaching of executives, I often spend a lot of time learning about this special relationship between leaders and their assistants. In some cases, I spend considerable time with the assistant to help optimize the relationship.

Below is a checklist of the type of things I ask or look for. (You'll see that many of the ideas come from chapter 3 on process that can be taken on by an effective EA.)

Calendar:

- Schedules power hours, maintains color coding

- Conducts look-aheads and blocks in vacations, days off, and important personal events

- Sets up recurring meetings including one-on-ones and esprit de corps efforts

Keeping day on track:

- Has schedule and files needed for the day organized and ready

- Protects the leader's first fifteen to thirty minutes of the day from people and meetings

- Where appropriate, pulls leader from meetings if running behind or puts fifteen-minute breaks in between meetings

Travel and expenses:

- Schedules travel and logistics with leader's preferences in mind

- Creates itinerary with all information in one place

- Handles all receipts and expense reports

Documents, systems, trackers:

- Populates information for commonly used templates in leader's role

- Inputs information into systems or trackers that leader must keep updated

- Helps to keep contacts updated

Personal (where negotiated):

- Helps with holiday cards

- Tracks personal birthdays and helps to send gifts/cards

- Schedules personal appointments

I've seen EAs become extensions of their leaders: skilled EAs capably represent their leaders in all contexts, interacting with the leaders' key constituencies in a way that extends the goodwill of their leaders and moves their agendas forward.[a]

When I have spoken to EAs who had great relationships with the leaders they supported, they shared that these folks took the extra steps to share context, explain who the key stakeholders were, and involve the EA as a critical member of the team. The leaders who gave their best received the best support in return.

a. Melba J. Duncan, "The Case for Executive Assistants," *Harvard Business Review*, May 2011, 88–91.

I want to acknowledge that this is all so much easier said than done. I know when I'm stressed by an urgent deliverable or when I'm feeling uncertain about something, my coping mechanism is the I'll Just Do It Myself Pitfall. Anxiety running high, I decide I'll just figure this out on my own and go for it. Controlling the situation gives me a temporary sense of relief, and sometimes it moves a task forward, but very often, bull-rushing a situation is the last thing the team needs from me. I am still learning to remember to pause, step back, and ask myself if this is something I *truly* need to insert myself into. Sometimes the answer may very well be yes. But if I conducted an audit of all the times I've succumbed to the I'll Just Do It Myself Pitfall, the truth is that probably more than 50 percent of the time I didn't need to get as involved in the way that I did.

You can end up doing yourself and your team a disservice when you step in and turn a task into a fire drill. It can leave a team feeling demotivated or give the impression you don't have confidence in them. The Leader A mindset, by contrast, is one of curiosity and confidence: your job is to help the team build the capability and the motivation to get there themselves. You want a team that functions interdependently while honoring each person's strengths and contributions.

Inspire: Move Beyond Just "Hub and Spoke." The inspire part of the leverage + empower + inspire equation takes the individual people you lead and helps them to feel part of a larger collective, vision, or mission. When I've done 360 reviews for folks, I've always been struck by those whose team members or employees describe being "willing to run through a brick wall" for the leader and the organization. When I probed more deeply, I found that the leader had not only leveraged and empowered the team but also had that final secret ingredient of being someone who inspired the team to connect their work to a meaningful goal.

This kind of leadership requires that you do more than just lead by "hub and spoke," where team members are connected to the larger whole mostly through their one-on-ones with you but don't necessarily feel connected to each other or the bigger picture. By leading point to point, you risk creating silos or creating perceptions of inner circles and favorites. Even worse, it can also become a time and energy sink if you're having five separate conversations when you could bring five people together for one decision.

Intentionally bring people together and build the esprit de corps of the group. For your organization, function, team, project, or initiative, ask yourself these questions:

- What is the vision or shared goal for the group?

- Who needs to be or feel included?

- How and by what cadence will you bring this group together?

- What are the collective wins that keep the momentum going?

- How will we all share in the success of this together?

One analogy I love when I think of leaders who are great at the inspire part of the leverage + empower + inspire equation is that of a crew team: all individuals working toward the same destination in perfect rhythm and harmony.

Legendary sportswriter Paul Gallico, who rowed for Columbia, beautifully described the bonding process a squad undergoes when it moves from a group of individuals to a single, unified crew. "We became one with the boat and our fellow oarsmen and felt ourselves as giants, since one's own power applied to the shell was multiplied by eight." According to Gallico, these moments bring "an ineffable delight" to the rowers, "a great exultation."[4]

This "great exultation" is known to oarsmen as *swing*. Swing is almost indescribable. It's the moment when eight individuals blend together and experience a feeling of transcendence as they glide effortlessly over the water as one. Writer Michael Socolow, who also rowed for Columbia, describes swing as "unity made manifest. It's surrender to process rather than demanding results."[5] When a crew is in a state of swing, individual ego and agenda falls away, and team members become a single unit whose effectiveness is far greater than the sum of its parts.

The parallels with effective business teams are easy to see. Individual team members must be highly skilled, self-reliant, and capable, but able to function as part of a synchronized group focused

BRING THE LEVERAGE + EMPOWER + INSPIRE EQUATION HOME

You can also use many of the concepts discussed so far to take a scan of your home and determine where you could gain more time, energy, and bandwidth. One colleague, a business owner and single mom, explained how she managed a big move with her two school-aged children to a new city:

I must tell you that I've really leaned on the "what's my highest and best use?" question at home! The move was more overwhelming than I anticipated—I really believed I could avoid any bumps in the road with superior organization. What I didn't factor in was all the things you can't anticipate, like unexpected repairs and my babysitter getting sick.

Point being, when I had one hundred things to do and felt like I had to do at least twenty of them simultaneously, I'd ask myself that question. Is it really my highest and best use to be unpacking this box of stuffed animals? Putting books on shelves? Mowing the lawn? And so on. Most of the time it was not, and these small tasks were things the kids could easily handle.

So I delegated anything I could to them. They learned all kinds of new things, gained confidence, and felt "important and adult." I was then free to work and tend to the big stuff, which left me much less stressed and therefore a better mom.

on the same goal. Peter Dean, writing for *Wharton Magazine*, observes that in rowing, "no member is the star of the team." Each one must (1) adapt to the strengths and shortcomings of the other, (2) empathize with the other's point of view, adjusting quickly to what's needed in the moment, (3) be open to every other member and willing to get past personal feelings of disappointment, and (4) give themselves up for the benefit of the entire crew, rowing as an extension of the teammate.[6] You could hardly ask for a better description of an effective team in the workplace!

Build a Strategic Network of Support

As you grow as a professional, you will have more responsibilities and pressures. It's increasingly difficult to get it all done on your own—or even with the team that reports to you.

To guard against the old adage "It gets lonelier at the top," be proactive in seeking support beyond your immediate team. This isn't the same kind of networking that you do when you're searching for jobs. These are the connections that help you be highly effective, present, and satisfied and that feed your Leader A.

To build that kind of network requires that you get more comfortable asking for help, find very specific types of support, and uphold your end of the relationship by being a good citizen and good support to others as well.

Get More Comfortable Asking for Help

It takes a fair amount of inner confidence and strength to admit that we need the advice or support of others. The *New York Times* article "Why Is Asking for Help So Difficult?" states that we don't ask because no one likes to seem weak, needy, or incompetent. Additionally, no one likes shifting the balance of power in a relationship where we feel like we are the one indebted to another person.[7]

Wayne Baker, author and faculty member at the University of Michigan's Ross School of Business, offers five concrete tips for getting better at asking for help:

1. KNOW EXACTLY WHAT YOU WANT TO ASK. Write down the specific steps and resources you need to achieve your goal and build your request for help upon them.

2. ASK SMARTLY. Make a request that is Specific, Meaningful (why you need it), Action-oriented (ask for something to be

done), Real (authentic, not made up), and Time-bound (when you need it).

3. DON'T ASSUME YOU KNOW WHO AND WHAT PEOPLE KNOW. You never know about other people's connections and insights until you ask! You can miss huge opportunities if you assume someone doesn't have the knowledge to help or interest in doing so.

4. BE PROACTIVE IN HELPING OTHERS. The spirit of reciprocity is so hardwired in our brains that more often than not, when we extend help to others, we can expect to receive help in return.

5. CREATE A CULTURE WHERE ASKING FOR HELP IS ENCOUR-AGED. Make it easy for your team members to ask for and extend help by setting the example. An environment where others give and receive help creates a feeling of psychological safety and normalizes the practice.[8]

We're all better off when we're able to be vulnerable enough to acknowledge our need for help and ask for it.

Reach Out to the Right People

Next, it's important to think strategically about the specific kind of support you need and who can fit the bill. The following isn't an exhaustive list but rather an illustration of the type of roles that others can play in your life if you look for them and allow them in under the tent.

Other experts: While you might be an expert in your own right, it's critical to seek out those who bring different experiences, understanding, and pattern recognition to the issues you're facing. This can include peers or even direct reports who have certain functional expertise that's critical for the year ahead, or external folks who have successfully navigated similar situations.

As you seek out the help of other experts, hold confidence in your own expertise while also adopting a *beginner's mind*. Beginner's mind is a term that comes from Zen Buddhism and refers to someone with an openness to learning, even at an advanced level. It's all about having an open attitude and stance.

In 2013 when Chip Conley was tapped to help develop Airbnb into the world's leading hospitality brand, he'd already spent more than twenty years as the founder and CEO of Joie de Vivre Hospitality, the second-largest boutique hotel brand in the United States, and was a *New York Times* best-selling author of titles such as *Peak: How Great Companies Get Their Mojo from Maslow*. But at Airbnb he found himself in unfamiliar territory: twice the age of the average employee and two decades older than CEO Brian Chesky, Conley had never worked in tech and had never even used Uber or Google Docs. Conley recognized he had a choice: walk away from his new job, or embrace beginner's mind in order to adapt and change. He decided to stay.[9]

Conley found a ready ally in Chesky, who was also a proponent of beginner's mind, and who, like Conley, saw a growth opportunity for both of them. Conley needed to learn the landscape and lingo of tech, while Chesky needed to learn from Conley's management experience and emotional intelligence. They bonded over their belief that anyone of any age can have a growth mindset, and Airbnb benefited from their "mutual mentorship." During the four years Conley worked full-time for the company, Airbnb expanded exponentially and garnered guest satisfaction reviews that surpassed the hotel industry's.[10]

A beginner's mind helps us to innovate and connect the dots during those moments when we engage and listen with openness. Watch out for trying to protect an idealized image of the expert who has all the answers. Trying to emphasize your expertise or even getting defensive about your need for help is exhausting, and it can preclude the very thing you need, which is support and new learning. True confidence is about knowing what you bring to the table while still having the humility to be blown away by another person's expertise and willing to entertain an insight or perspective that shapes your future thinking. As Zen master Shunryu Suzuki stated so well, "In the beginner's mind there are many possibilities, but in the expert's there are few."[11]

Sausage makers: As you become more senior, there is a premium on being clear, concise, and articulate. For some of us, it takes processing out loud to get to that kind of clarity and conviction. This kind of rough, unedited processing isn't meant for public consumption— hence the term *sausage making,* as no one really cares to see how sausage is made! If you're someone who needs to talk things out to get to clarity, know with whom you can talk through big decisions, difficult conversations, or presentations. This kind of sounding board will help you frame key messages or communications.

Don't go to those who lack the patience to be a sounding board, or even worse, don't go to the people who weigh in on your performance evaluations. Without an understanding of what you need, they may unintentionally peg you as someone who is not articulate, who isn't fact-based or logical, or who wastes their time. If you must make sausage with anyone who holds a position to evaluate you, be sure to preface it by saying, "I'd love to brainstorm something with you," or "This thought isn't fully formed yet, but I wonder if I could get your gut reaction before I have the team substantiate it with additional data."

Accountability buddies: For our most important goals or objectives, it can be helpful to have someone other than your boss or the board holding you accountable. This is someone who knows what you want to achieve and helps you get there by checking in on milestones. These people can help you keep your eye on the big rocks. I learned the term *accountability buddy* from one of the CEOs I coached who shared that the sole reason he was hiring me was to help ensure he stayed focused on the strategic vision, key priorities, and collective wins for his organization.

Once someone agrees to be your accountability buddy, come up with a check-in system that makes the most sense for what you're trying to achieve and for both of your schedules. Also decide on the format for your meetings. Quarterly check-ins may be fine for long-term strategic goals, but I've had clients who met with their accountability partner on a monthly basis, and some who've done weekly check-ins when they had a tight deadline or wanted to make quicker progress.

Mirrors: As you take on more senior roles, you might find there are fewer people who are willing to give it to you straight, call you out, or hold you accountable to the purpose and vision you've set. It's always important to have someone who can identify your blind spots and reflect back to you what they see, like a mirror. Who's the "straight talker" in your life whose insights you can trust? This could be a person in your organization you've known for many years or a person not at all connected to your industry, who has no personal stake in your organization.

Helicopters: While some people are detail-oriented and excel at focusing on the granular level, helicopters are those who provide an aerial view, help you see the world differently, or help you to connect your daily work to the bigger picture or a longer-term horizon. These are folks who help to strengthen your thinking on an issue by offering you benchmarks, pointing out trade-offs to consider, or raising the organizational or market conditions at play. They help you see the future impact and implications on different groups by widening perspective—a key characteristic of Leader A mode. Look for the people who think big—or at least think differently than you do. A different perspective can move you forward or trigger a breakthrough when you're stuck in a rut.

Cheerleaders: Who doesn't need a cheerleader from time to time? When we're working hard, an "attaboy" or "attagirl" can go a long way to keep energy and motivation alive. Know who you can turn to when you need acknowledgment, a pep talk, or a pat on the back. If you don't instinctively know who this person is, ask yourself: Who can I count on to notice and affirm that I am adding value? Who can share a victory lap with me? Who is genuinely happy for me when I hit a major deliverable, have a presentation go well, or have a great aha moment?

It's heartbreaking when I see a client seeking acknowledgment or reassurance from people who fundamentally lack the patience, capacity, or even the capability to do this. Precious energy is wasted in counterproductive efforts to get acknowledgment from that one boss or one colleague who absolutely is not wired to give it to you. Focus instead on the people in your life who naturally support, love, or acknowledge your efforts in meaningful ways.

Safe harbors: In a similar vein, rather than focus energy on people who are negative, toxic, or self-absorbed, learn to channel your efforts into those who fundamentally respect you and have the emotional intelligence required to be a safe harbor. Psychological safety is an important dimension of both individual and team performance. Research from Harvard Business School professor Amy Edmondson has shown that we optimize performance and learning in groups when both accountability and safety are present.[12] With whom can you let your guard down and share your ideas, thoughts, and observations without judgment or retribution? As your ideas percolate, who will listen and consider the possibilities without raining on your parade or trying to one-up you? That's your safe harbor.

As you consider these seven roles, remember that it's not necessary to find people to match *all* of them. You may have a couple of people who are able to fulfill multiple roles—or you may find that your situation requires only one or two of them. But as you look for the best folks to bring under the tent, consider colleagues, friends, contacts, or family members. If you can't find someone in your own circle, you might find that bringing in the additional support of an executive coach, a therapist, or a wellness trainer is just what you need.

EXERCISE

Assess Your Current Strategic Network of Support

- Consider the strength of your strategic network of support. Who could you add to help you feed Leader A and maintain your highest and best?

TABLE 4-2

Assess your current strategic network of support

Role	Who's playing this role in my life now?	Who could play it?	Who could I play this role for at work or in my personal life?
Expert			
Sausage maker			
Accountability buddy			
Mirror			
Helicopter			
Cheerleader			
Safe harbor			

- To whom do you offer that same support?

- Use table 4-2 to answer these questions and assess your network of support.

Be a Good Citizen

As you assemble your network of support, be careful not to adopt a "take" mentality. Wharton professor Adam Grant has explored the roles of "givers" and "takers" in his research. Givers contribute to others with no expectation of receiving anything in return. Takers, meanwhile, try to get others to serve their needs while guarding their own expertise and time.[13] We've all been on the receiving end of people who made audacious requests or who call us only when they need something, or who may give but with a quid pro quo mentality. We've all rolled our eyes at the people who are suddenly nice and charming when they need something or believe there is some commercial gain or benefit in it for them.

In contrast, the best supportive relationships evince a healthy give-and-take of information, social access and connections, and personal time and energy.[14] In the *New York Times Magazine* article "What Google Learned from Its Quest to Build the Perfect

Team," researchers found that a feeling of "psychological safety" was the most important component for ensuring that a team was successful and worked well together. Amy Edmondson's work that I mentioned was a critical underpinning to what the Google research found. High-performance teams are characterized by interpersonal trust, mutual respect, conversational turn-taking, and empathy.[15] In relationships like these we see that powerful virtuous cycle of growth at work, where we're aligned to core fundamental values of generosity, service, and nonjudgment. Sometimes our relationships and our desire to support others outweigh time efficiency or productivity because it's just the right thing to do.

Here are some tips to keep in mind as you build a community of support in a thoughtful and generative way:

- BE A CONSISTENT PRESENCE: There's nothing more aggravating than someone who is normally impatient and curt and suddenly becomes charming and friendly when they need something. Instead, be available consistently, with a positive presence.

- REMEMBER TO ACKNOWLEDGE AND EXPRESS GRATITUDE: A simple "thank-you" goes a long way.

- FOLLOW UP AND INFORM: Let the other person know how you used information they gave or synthesized what you learned from them, or let them know if you've connected with a contact they offered.

- BE AWARE OF RELATIONSHIP OWNERSHIP: Don't take for granted the social capital someone else may have expended for you.

- LOOK FOR OPPORTUNITIES TO GIVE BACK: Consider how you can play one of the seven roles I've mentioned for someone else. Pay it forward.

A WORD ON YOUR HOME TEAM

When it comes to teams and personal support networks, think beyond work and don't forget your home team. Teams at home can be defined in many ways and may include your partner, kids, parents, cousins, closest friends, boyfriend/girlfriends, and pets.

Don't assume those closest to us will give us a pass. Our loved ones tend to be more lenient and more forgiving because they love us, but we can't make the mistake of always giving them our worst. As I've already mentioned, a cue for many leaders that Leader B mode is taking over is when they find themselves lashing out at their loved ones and taking out work stress on them. Therefore, one of the big things I encourage you to consider is that your team at home—those who are most dear to us—also deserves your best.

Ask yourself what kind of support they need. For example, give them the courtesy of communication. Give them a heads-up when new things arise, and involve them in the big decisions about career changes or major projects or dream goals you hope to take on. Consider how these things will affect the whole of your life and your home team.

For many of the folks I work with, we come up with a team name. One leader named his family "Team Quinn" after his last name. Each week, we talked not just about what happened at work but also what was going on with Team Quinn. Once he got behind the concept of Team Quinn, he started to get more involved in family life. He began coaching his son's basketball team, for example. He had always assumed his wife would give him a pass, but she had been an incredible source of support and help all these years, and now he wanted to spend more intentional time with family. He gave himself more permission to truly enjoy vacations, to work less, and to focus on his home team in a different way.

Establish Boundaries and Rules of Engagement

For some of you, the strategic network of support exercise might yield a different insight entirely. Perhaps you realize that *you* are that person who plays these roles for others. You are in service of others and always putting others' needs ahead of your own. If this is you, know that in addition to learning to allow yourself to receive the support of others, there is also opportunity for more Leader A days by building more effective boundaries and shifting your rules of engagement with others—especially in today's work environment, where collaboration is so prized.

One leader, Derek, felt he was constantly in demand from his team, his peers, and his boss. Someone was always stopping by his office to ask a question or seek advice. As a natural "cheerleader" and "safe harbor" for others, he valued being sought after for counsel. But on the other hand, his schedule was constantly interrupted and his projects were continually derailed—so much so that by the end of a typical day, he felt frustrated and exhausted. Derek regularly fell into the I'll Just Do It Later Pitfall because other people's demands and needs kept coming in front of his own top priorities and self-care. It was time for Derek to update his boundaries and rules of engagement. Following are some ways he did so.

Practice Bringing Attention to Your Own Needs

When you're in a situation like Derek's, and the people around you are not shy to declare, ask for, or put their own needs first, it's easy to lose sight of your own. Healthy relationships and boundaries come first, with a greater understanding of where your own needs begin and end and where others' needs begin and end.

For example, try this experiment. Take a sheet of paper and draw a horizontal line across the middle. Now, above the line, write down everything that is a true need or priority that originates solely from you. Then, below the line on the bottom half of the page, write down all the requests, emails you must return, documents you're working on, or things you have on the list that are *in response to* someone else's needs or requests, including those of your team, boss, clients/customers, friends, and so on.

I know it's not totally black and white given all the interdependencies we have with others, but give it a try for the sake of being able to see where your priorities and needs begin and end and where others' priorities and needs begin and end. Here are some of the things I hear from clients, like Derek, who try this exercise:

- When I looked at what was on the bottom half of the sheet, I realized out of sheer habit, I tend to handle those items first.

- While I'm responsive to others, I risk never getting to some of the important longer-term items on the top half of the page.

- I was surprised by how uncomfortable the experiment was. It felt selfish to make that kind of distinction between my needs and others' needs.

- I could feel the part of me that likes to be wanted, wants to be connected to others, doesn't want to let others down. But maybe I've taken it too far by always putting the top half of the paper off to later.

Another good way to start practicing paying attention to your own needs is noticing when you are starting to feel "quietly" frustrated, resentful, angry, or upset about something. When you feel this tension, immediately get curious:

- Do I have an unspoken expectation or need I'm not expressing?

- Is there a request of someone else I'm not making that I need to?

- Am I watering down what I really need by not wanting to trouble others?

- What is the underlying need I have?

THE COST OF INEFFECTIVE BOUNDARIES

Consider this sobering reality: research from leaders across twenty organizations shows that those considered valued sources of information and those most in demand by others have the lowest career satisfaction over time.

Women often bear the most penalties:

- The lion's share of collaborative work tends to fall to women, who are expected to help others with heavy workloads, provide mentoring and training, and recruit or attend optional meetings.

- Men are 36 percent more likely to share knowledge and expertise; they're considered an informational resource. Women are 66 percent more likely to assist others in need, an action that costs more time and energy.

- Men who stayed late to help colleagues earned 14 percent higher ratings than women who did the same. When neither helped, women were rated 12 percent lower than men.

Source: Rob Cross, Reb Rebele, and Adam Grant, "Collaborative Overload," *Harvard Business Review*, January–February 2016, https://hbr.org/2016/01/collaborative -overload.

Be Clear on Emotional Ownership and Accountability

I'm not suggesting that you stop supporting others or stop being in service of others. I'm asking you to give yourself permission to ac-knowledge your own priorities and to take accountability for them, and to recognize when others have needs and when they—not you—need to take accountability for them. Here are some strategies to try.

Discern when giving is about your values rather than about your fears. As I continued to work with Derek, he and I dug more deeply into the dynamics at his work and discovered the difference between a Leader A and a Leader B day. On Leader A days, Derek gave or supported someone else in a way that left him feeling like he had truly made a difference or contributed to someone else meaningfully. The "give" was authentic and sincere, and it tied to his core values of good citizenship, generosity, and using his gifts, talents, and natural emotional intelligence wisely.

As Derek reflected on Leader B days, he saw that some of the motivation behind his giving or responding to others was to avoid conflict or preclude guilt. He realized the people most getting his attention were often the loudest, pushiest, or whiniest, or those who backed him up on his heels. On those Leader B days, he felt manipulated or fearful of someone else's retribution, disappointment, or disapproval.

Add EO to your EQ. Emotional ownership (EO) is the ability to take responsibility and accountability for your own emotions. *Emotional quotient* (EQ) is the ability to tune into others. Maybe, like Derek, you have great EQ—and in fact, your antennae for others' feelings may be so powerful that you absorb too much, beyond what is yours. You may be unnecessarily taking on more stress or accountability for that other person than the situation warrants.

When your EQ is high, you may be able to sense others' emotions, needs, or desires (maybe even before they are able to articulate them!), but part of the work is learning to notice them without reacting, giving in, or rescuing (we'll cover more on this in chapter 5 on presence). When you feel the urge to say yes to another person or take on something for them, but you know you are doing it out of fear or habit rather than your values, hit the pause button. Say to yourself before acting: "This is their emergency, not mine." You can also use the power of visualization: imagine pulling your antennae back into yourself when they start to feel frayed. Give yourself a break from always sensing what's going on for others.

Respond with Grace

When I work with people on building healthier boundaries, I caution them not to swing the pendulum too far the other way. This can lead to a disruption and inconsistency of presence—especially if your demeanor is naturally approachable and open.

Boundaries are not about putting on a suit of armor and assuming a defensive posture in trying to protect your time, energy, or emotions like a solider stationed at the top of a fortress keeping enemies at bay. They're also not about opening your door so wide that everyone and anything can get in. They're about finding that middle ground that honors and protects your needs while remaining judiciously available to others. Figure 4-2 provides a visual of the continuum of boundaries; the goal is to aim for the middle ground of "Healthy Boundaries."

Seek more information and assess. Hear out another person's need and then assess the situation: Is that a need you can meet authentically? There are no hard-and-fast rules. Because there is always nuance in situations, rather than a default yes or a default no, don't give an answer right away. If the request comes via email, ask to set up a time to hear out the person or send some questions to clarify what's really being asked. Solicit the information you need so you can make an astute decision for your organization, your family, or yourself. Now go back to chapter 2 and look at the categories of your yesses and nos. Seek information to determine if this is a *strategic yes*, if this is a *partial yes*, or if it was *never your yes to begin with*.

Acknowledge the request or person. While you might be turning down or renegotiating the request itself, it doesn't mean you have to turn down the person. Remember, these interactions with others

FIGURE 4-2

Continuum of boundaries

Defensive boundaries	Rigid boundaries	Healthy boundaries	Porous boundaries	Poor/no boundaries
Suit of armor	Aloof, protective	Clear sense of self and others	Approachable	Enmeshed or codependent

are still points of connection, and important relationships should always be handled with care and respect. Make your goodwill transparent, and use your EQ to acknowledge what you sense may be going on for the other person:

- "I appreciate your thinking of me for this opportunity."

- "I hear your sense of urgency on this."

- "That is a good question."

- "While I can't do it myself, I'm happy to refer you to some others who may be a good fit."

Respond accordingly. How you ultimately respond then becomes a function of how you assessed the situation or request. Below are a range of possible responses:

- SAY NO GRACIOUSLY WITHOUT DEFENSIVENESS: There are some cases where taking a pass or politely declining a request or an invitation is what is most important for your long-term effectiveness and scalability. Consider the trade-offs or implications of saying yes to one additional thing that could tip the scales.

- SHARE WHAT YOU CAN DO: In some cases, we are able to assist but not for the whole need. Offer what you can do, or let the person know when you would become available. Share the conditions by which you'd be able to help, and make that be a starting point to negotiate a win-win.

- OFFER SUGGESTIONS OR ALTERNATIVES: Help make the connection to the right person on your team. You could say something like: "Given what you are trying to solve, it's best to speak to Henry, who's closer to that issue," or "Out of respect to the team, George would be your best person to help you sort that through," or "You'll get a speedier outcome by going to Maria on that."

- SHARE ADDITIONAL CONTEXT IF WARRANTED: Name the risks and trade-offs to other potential projects or engagements if you take on the request. You want all parties to understand the impact on you, the work, or the other person. Share your assumptions about where something sits in the broader set of priorities for the team or the organization.

Understand that your relationships with other people are a dance and that as you grow and take on new things, you will outgrow certain people or relationships. As you change the rules of engagement, there could be backlash or discomforts. That is why I encourage you not to swing the pendulum too far and to always act in alignment to your character and values, with what's best for the business and strategic for the situation at hand.

The Last Word on People

Having an underperforming team, a lack of key head count, or conflict with others at work are some of the quickest, and perhaps most painful, ways to fall into Leader B mode. When one member of a team suffers or slips into a pitfall, the entire team is adversely affected. However, the converse is true, and a team that enjoys psychological safety and works well together is far more effective and satisfied than the sum of its parts, leading to more Leader A days for everyone.

Our work lives will always be intertwined with and dependent on many different people, and many different types of people. Especially as your impact expands, you'll need to lean more on the support of your people in order to meet your personal goals and the goals of the organization. When people are all working together at their highest and best, the resulting synergy can lead to incredible results and long-term effectiveness and satisfaction for everyone involved.

What to Remember:

➤ People are a direct contributing factor to our Leader A mode when they bring the capacity, energy, and support needed to meet a deadline, realize a big goal, or build a company with great success and scale. On the other hand, people can be a contributing factor to Leader B when a key role on your team is empty or when you feel drained by your interactions with others.

> A Leader A mindset is critical to becoming comfortable with depending on others, which requires that we ask for help and see the unique value and contributions our colleagues bring. At the same time, a Leader A mindset helps us maintain healthy boundaries and rules of engagement so people don't drain our energy. We are able to care for ourselves as well as for others.

> You can raise your game while raising the game of others by taking a good hard look at the teams you lead, either directly or indirectly. Regularly examine the strength, structure, and composition of your team, making sure you have the right people on the bus. Get ahead of the curve on succession planning so you set in place a virtuous cycle: as you continue to grow and free yourself to take on new things, you are helping your people free up and take on new things, and then they in turn can help others grow and take on new things. As you move from being a leader of tasks to leader of a team to a leader of leaders, continually optimize the way you leverage, empower, and inspire those you work with.

> Don't take for granted the reality of taking on expanded or new roles. As accountabilities, performance pressures, and high-stake situations increase, the age-old adage of "It gets lonelier at the top" becomes more real. Build a strategic network of support to ensure you have what you need for both your performance and well-being by getting more comfortable asking for help, considering the types of people you need to support your leadership and life (experts, sausage makers, accountability buddies, mirrors, helicopters, cheerleaders, and safe harbors), and remembering to play those roles for others.

➤ If you find that you support others to the point of stress, exhaustion, or feeling overwhelmed, look at your current boundaries and rules of engagement. This will mean getting increasingly comfortable with bringing attention to your own needs, being clear on what is actually yours to own in terms of emotions and accountabilities, and learning to hold boundaries and respond to incoming requests with greater grace and clarity.

CHAPTER FIVE

The Power of Presence
Don't Scratch the Itch

Yasmina had built a successful career as an independent HR consultant. While she wanted to continue working in the field and loved the autonomy associated with owning and running her own business, she felt her career had plateaued. Over the years she'd toyed with the possibility of expanding by adding subcontractors, as she found herself routinely turning away potential clients. But even more than she wanted to grow her business, Yasmina wanted to grow personally by building greater visibility and a brand for herself, perhaps by starting to blog and speak at conferences. Yet each time she cleared out space and sat down to work on her own brand, her inner critic kicked in: "You can barely keep up now; how do you think you're going to take on another thing? There are a million blogs out there already—why would anyone be interested in yours? Just stick with what you know." With this kind of inner monologue always in play, Yasmina found herself perpetually procrastinating when it came to developing her own brand.

Despite a deep understanding of the greater sense of purpose that was beckoning her, and even some specific milestones she wanted to hit—speaking at conferences, blogging, eventually writing a book—Yasmina was stuck in a pattern of self-sabotage. Deep down she knew she had the goods to build a brand *and* to expand her business if she chose to. But after years of habitually putting off her dreams, she was stuck in the rut of procrastination—not to mention stuck in Leader B mode, despite having a successful business. To get back to Leader A and start working on her own brand, which would offer her the passion and contribution she was missing, Yasmina realized something needed to change.

The Impact of Presence on Leader A and Leader B

We've all been in Yasmina's shoes. We want to make progress on a goal, whether it's an external deliverable like hitting a sales goal, completing a project, or launching a new product, or an internal aim such as allocating time to work on strategy, spending less time on the road, or getting to the gym. But despite a strong desire, it seems we can't move that goal forward for the life of us. We know what it is we want to do or achieve, but it's as if something takes over and we just can't help ourselves in reverting right back to what we've always done. My dear friend and fellow executive coach, Pam Krulitz, describes these moments as times we "want to scratch the itch."

In addition to our own habits and emotions sometimes impeding our momentum, staying focused and sustaining progress on a long-term goal is harder than ever in the world we live in, which is set up to pull on our attention and scatter our energy. Today's 24-7 technology and information overload inherently fragments our focus. Studies have shown that the average officer worker receives hundreds of emails a day and that even the buzz of a phone creates a decrease in productivity.[1] These types of distractions make it difficult to maintain attention and focus, and they make it all too easy to procrastinate. Our attention becomes split and fragmented, and we end up devoting more superficial attention to many things, rather than deep, sustained attention to the critical-path items.

This is where the fourth P, presence, comes to the rescue. Presence helps us to maintain the focus and attention needed to move forward important goals. It increases our emotional resilience to tolerate what may be uncomfortable in the short term so we can learn new patterns and practices that create and sustain long-term progress, and it builds our inner capacity to pause and make more thoughtful, wise decisions.

Therefore, in this chapter, I'll lay out ways to hack and break the patterns of behavior that impede our effectiveness and don't support Leader A—those behaviors that we always later regret. I'll start by sharing ways to quickly get present and stay focused when distraction or procrastination gets the better of you. Then, I'll share a practice I use with my clients to help put them into virtuous cycles of success while breaking outdated and reactive patterns that burn up energy, waste time, and lead to ineffectiveness and dissatisfaction. You'll learn how to find and extend the "pause" time between stimulus and response, increasing the probability that you won't "scratch the itch" when things get tough and instead will be able to choose a leadership action or the leadership voice best suited for the situation at hand.

Get Present and Stay Focused

As a goal-driven professional, Yasmina loved thinking about each new summit to reach. However, this time, as she looked out into the distant horizon at all the ways she wanted to grow her personal brand, everything felt too risky, too big, and too overwhelming. In fact, looking at the totality of all the challenges ahead was so overwhelming it was a large part of what led to her habit of procrastination and self-sabotage. To avoid becoming overwhelmed, Yasmina needed ways to zoom in and keep things at the manageable, bite-sized level. As I shared in chapter 3 on process, sometimes reaching a larger goal requires "brushing your teeth on it" just a little bit each day.

Here are some tips and tactics to help stay focused and in action the next time you feel especially distracted or find yourself procrastinating.

Work Off-line

The next time you need to work on something important that demands your full attention, set limits by working off-line. Especially during your power hours (chapter 3), turn off notifications or even turn off internet access if that keeps you from being tempted. If you are in a meeting that you've predetermined serves your highest and best use (chapter 2), then give the meeting and your colleagues your full attention by putting your phone on airplane mode and closing your laptop.

Take Single Steps

Bring your focus from the mountain to the molehill. In other words, attend to one and only one step at a time until the task is complete. If you start to think of all the things you must get done and the sheer volume starts to feel overwhelming, gently bring your attention back to the present moment, the current step. You can only do one step at a time anyway, so give each successive one your full presence and your highest and best effort. As Lao Tzu said, the journey of a thousand miles begins with a single step.

Give Yourself Fifteen Minutes to Get into It

If you find yourself avoiding tasks or really resistant to a project, you can say to yourself: "I just need to get through the first fifteen minutes." As with exercising—a challenge for many of us—the first fifteen to twenty minutes are often the hardest. But if you can get yourself over that initial hump, you'll eventually realize you've hit a point of deep focus and flow. You may even start to enjoy the feeling of getting something done and genuinely get into the task you were dreading.

Stay Anchored in the Physical

If you find that even after fifteen to twenty minutes, tolerating the discomfort isn't working and you're still drawn to surf the Web, check your email, or get up for a third snack, try anchoring yourself in something physical. Your head is trying to convince you how terrible and onerous this task is, so aim to get out of your head and into your body. A few examples include:

- Literally look down at your hands at the keyboard and feel your fingers tap each key.

- Feel your feet on the floor. If it's possible, take a moment or two to feel your feet in your shoes or on the ground.

- Notice where your body contacts your chair.

- Bring attention to how you are sitting. Shift your position if necessary to ensure good posture.

- Sit up straight and take a few deep breaths.

- Imagine lifting your chest up to the sky, creating a little more openness and space, then keep going.

Use a Grounding Visualization Technique

You can also use a visualization technique to bring your attention and focus to the body. One great example of this comes from Loren Shuster, chief people officer at the Lego Group, who explained that when he has important meetings or presentations, he takes five minutes to ground himself in his body by visualizing coming fully alive in each cell. "When you're not grounded, when you're not connected to your body and surrounding environment," he says, "you don't have a strong sense of direction or purpose. You're just floating. The smallest thing can distract you. This grounding technique helps me clear my mind, recharge my energy, strengthen my instincts, and calm my emotions."[2]

Break Vicious Cycles and Create Virtuous Ones

These tips can help to address the immediate symptoms of distraction or procrastination. Other times, you may find that like Yasmina, you need to work more at the root-cause level to see if there is a pattern at play that makes it hard to break a bad habit. If this is the case, the next step is to increase your capacity to get present to and tolerate a wider range of emotions and discomforts. In effect, you're widening your comfort zone. We live in the kind of world where we are seduced into thinking we are supposed to be happy all the time and, on top of that, constantly perform as supermen or superwomen. Thus, when we experience an unpleasant feeling—sadness, anxiety, loneliness, disappointment, or self-criticism, for example—we try to escape what we dislike and move toward what feels good. This is a natural tendency, but if we get in the habit of avoiding every difficult feeling or being effective only when we're in our comfort zone and things feel good, we can get trapped in unproductive reactive patterns of distraction, perfectionism, procrastination, or rumination. For example, I am someone who generally does not like conflict with others, so I risk avoiding difficult conversations. If I'm not careful, I end up ruminating about the situation rather than doing something about it. By increasing my tolerance of the anxiety that conflict brings me and being able to stay present even in the face of this kind of discomfort, I've preserved my sense of choice and agency.

To stop this kind of self-sabotage, consider these three steps of a practice I use with clients that can help you to get present, find and break old patterns, and then create new choices and pathways to Leader A:

- STEP 1: SPECTATE: Observe yourself and see the patterns at play.

- STEP 2: REGULATE: Find the pause and don't scratch the itch.

- STEP 3: ADAPT: Realize the power of choice and create new if-thens.

Step 1: Spectate: Observe Yourself and See the Patterns at Play

In the introduction, I talked about the idea of being a spectator and being able to observe yourself while in action. Now we return to that concept and focus on how to build this capability further.

Move from Self-Aware to Spectator-Aware. As we've discussed, self-awareness is a critical part of leadership and coming to understand what feeds your own version of Leader A. Now, let's be clear on what distinguishes what I call "spectator-aware" from just "self-aware." There are three defining characteristics:

1. YOU ARE IMPARTIAL AND NONJUDGMENTAL. Spectating is *impartial*. Its fundamental purpose is to observe yourself and your experiences—not to blame, explain, criticize, or make excuses. This kind of self-observation constitutes the foundation of mindfulness. Jon Kabat-Zinn, PhD, widely considered the godfather of contemporary mindfulness practice, has described mindfulness as one's ability to assume the "stance of an impartial witness to your own experience." He says we must always practice mindfulness "with an attitude of non-judgment."[3]

2. YOU MAKE WHAT IS SUBJECTIVE MORE OBJECTIVE. Spectator-awareness is more powerful than self-awareness because as you maintain an impartial stance, you are increasing your ability to take what is normally a subjective thing— yourself (the subject) and your thoughts, emotions, actions, and experiences—and become open to examining them in an objective and nondefensive way. Bob Kegan and Lisa Laskow Lahey at the Harvard Graduate School of Education describe this as building *subject-object capability*. This is our ability to "stand back from [our] own filter and look at it, not just through it."[4] The analogy that Kegan and Lahey give is that it's like taking an X-ray of a person's thoughts and actions and putting it in front of them to review.[5]

3. YOU GAIN BETTER DATA BY WHICH TO DETERMINE FUTURE
ACTIONS. As with any business problem or challenge, the
best leaders gather data, run appropriate analyses, and then
make effective decisions. In effect, spectating involves doing
the same thing, but now you're gathering data on yourself
and your experience for the sake of building better leadership
mindsets, choices, and subsequent behaviors. Ronald Heifetz
and Marty Linsky, authors of *Adaptive Leadership* and
Leadership on the Line, call this a leader's ability to get off
the dance floor and go to the balcony. As they describe it, it's
a chance to step back from the action and ask, what's really
going on here?[6]

This ability to step out of the action and be a spectator to our own
experience is one of the chief skills I help my clients build. It's a core
component of the fourth P, presence, and an essential skill for feeding
Leader A. One leader recently shared this with me: "One of the most
important things in life is making a central contribution to a mission
greater than oneself. Our own behaviors interfere with mission. What
are our behaviors and habits which interfere with leading? We won't
have a clue until we can take an honest look at ourselves."

Build Your Spectating Muscle. The ability to make what is normally a subject (ourselves) an object may sound a little strange and
esoteric at first, but it's actually a skill you can practice and improve. Here are a couple of ways to become better at building your
spectating muscle.

Write it all down. One method is to write down your experience as
close to when it's happening in real time. You get a dual benefit
here: pausing to write can stop you from having a mindless reaction that you'll later regret, and if you're diligent in recording your
experience, you'll eventually have a great set of data to mine for
fully understanding your patterns. One client used this technique
in the following way: whenever something started to bother him,
he would send himself or me an email to capture his thoughts in
real time. Some good questions you can ask yourself include:

- What was the trigger when I had an "I just can't help myself" moment?

- What were the emotions I experienced?

- What was the voice track (or inner commentary) in my mind?

- What body sensations did I experience?

- What was my response to the moment—what did I do?

Debrief with another person. If you are more extroverted or find it helpful to hear yourself talk out loud, in addition to writing you can also enlist the help of another person to reflect and process out loud what is happening. If you do, it's important to do so with someone who fits the category of "safe harbor" or "sausage maker" from chapter 4 on people.

Identify the triggers. One thing I always ask the folks I work with to track is their triggers, or the stimuli that elicited their personal "scratch-the-itch" response. Author and noted leadership and resilience speaker Anne Grady explains that triggers are the things that cause us to have a knee-jerk response to a situation. When we're triggered, the emotional part of our brain takes over, and the logical brain takes a back seat. In this state, we "lose the ability to solve problems, make decisions, and think rationally . . . and to see things as they really are." But when we take the time to be a spectator to our own experience, we not only move out of this state of being "emotionally hijacked" and regain the ability to see clearly; we also gain awareness of what our particular triggers are. Armed with that knowledge, we can begin to manage how we choose to react to our triggers.[7]

One professional, Stefan, began working on picking his battles more effectively rather than frequently getting into conflict with others. He said it was amazing to see the "arc" of how his stress played out, and that usually by day 2, he could get to the other side of things. Seeing the pattern reflected in his own writing saved Stefan many a potential conflict with colleagues. Where he previously would have jumped in immediately, litigating everything and trying to win, Stefan learned to step back, take stock, and let the situation play out a little longer when he felt triggered. Once out of this state of high reactivity, he could see more clearly and interact with colleagues more calmly. (And it's worth noting that, as we see here with Stefan, sometimes the best reaction is simply *not* to react immediately.)

EXERCISE

Have You Been SCARFed?

One very helpful model to add to your spectating toolbox is the SCARF model created by David Rock, director of the NeuroLeadership Institute and author of *Your Brain at Work*. Rock and his team have found that there are five primary needs we all have (see column one in the following table).[8] When we perceive that any of these needs are threatened, a trigger occurs that can lead to a Leader B mindset. These can be helpful to better understand your own needs or the needs of others you are managing, mentoring, or coaching. The second column describes each part of SCARF, and the third column provides real-life examples of what this trigger looks like. Read through it and think about which are most important to you and which are most easily threatened.

TABLE 5-1

The SCARF table

SCARF need	Description	Examples of a SCARF need that may be threatened or triggered
Status	The need for others to show respect for . . . • Your competence, capability, or expertise • Your relationships, political capital, or power	• You don't feel your expertise is being valued because you felt unheard in a meeting • You say yes to taking on an extra position for something outside of work because it is prestigious, even though you don't really have the time • You get angry at more junior team members who don't respond to you immediately

SCARF need	Description	Examples of a SCARF need that may be threatened or triggered
Certainty	The need for information or direction that increases . . . • An understanding of timing or greater clarity on a plan • A sense of predictability, order, and structure	• Your boss or colleague just changed the deadline—again—on something you are working on • The organization has announced a reorganization, and now you feel your position could be at risk • The promotion process in your organization feels like a "black box"—no one seems to be able to give a clear answer on whether you will make partner or not
Autonomy	The need for a . . . • Sense of control • Sense of ownership	• Your boss just swooped in and has gotten involved in something you thought you were the lead on • You operate in a partnership with peers who are slow to make decisions that try to drive everyone to consensus
Relatedness	The need for . . . • Goodwill, rapport, and relationship • Acknowledgment or cheerleading	• You are working with a colleague who is transactional, short on time, and impatient and doesn't seem interested in you • Your boss shares constructive feedback but rarely gives kudos for a job well done
Fairness	The need for . . . • A sense of meritocracy • Feeling like performance is valued	• You see someone get promoted who you feel doesn't deserve it • You work in a culture where people play politics and try to be part of the inner circle or club

The issue is not that you have any of these needs. In fact, part of Leader A is knowing what your needs are and then having the personal sense of agency to get them met. However, we're in danger of Leader B mode when we're not present to the need, get triggered because it's been threatened, take things personally, or get overly reactive, which leads to ineffective decisions.

Using the SCARF model, you can have a better understanding of what needs aren't being met and why you're being triggered. This will help you not scratch the itch or react without thinking.

Notice the Voice Track and Physiological Patterns. In addition to collecting data on your triggers, you will also want to understand both the corresponding *voice track*, or your internal monologue, and the physiological contractions at the moment when you want to scratch the itch.

For example, Yasmina used a journaling exercise to observe and record her internal reactions and the accompanying voice track that came up each time she thought about her visions for the future. After a couple of weeks of this exercise, a clear pattern emerged. Anytime she felt fear and stress, she responded by finding anything else to work on other than the one thing she most wanted to work on. And while she felt a little embarrassed at first to admit this, she shared that the inner dialogue in her mind sounded like a scolding parent: "Who do you think you are? What if you fail? You're going to embarrass yourself." Her voice track came with an increased heart and breathing rate. Yasmina said it was helpful to observe what was happening rather than experience a generalized, vague sense of distress and self-doubt.

After catching on to her pattern, Yasmina said, "I can really see how once the anxiety and fear kick in, I fall right into the I'll Just Do It Later Pitfall. My stuff always gets put off while I'm waiting for some magical day when I'm totally on top of things and the timing seems perfect, or some imaginary day when *I* feel confident and perfect." For Yasmina, a sole proprietor, there would never be an end to the to-do list, and the quickest means of relief from her anxiety about expanding her brand was doing more client work. Busying herself with client work was her preferred form of procrastination, and it made perfect sense: because it was her job, after all, it was a fully legitimate way of immediately taking the attention off herself, and she was regularly rewarded in the form of positive feedback, referrals, and more opportunities.

Every person's patterns are different; the key is to self-spectate and objectively observe yours. One leader who was working on delegating more shared that his "spectating experiment," as he called it, led him to notice that he would feel a pit in his stomach anytime he wasn't in his comfort zone of high-volume activity. The corresponding voice track was really tempting: "Randy, wouldn't it feel good to respond to that email or head into the detail here?" As he connected the dots by naming all these things aloud, he discovered that beneath his physical discomfort and the I'll Just Do It Myself Pitfall was an underlying fear of letting go of things he was really good at.

Another client named Natalie shared that self-spectating led her to notice that she felt her jaw tighten and her blood pressure rise most acutely when someone on her team didn't perform. The voice track said, "This person is so incompetent! How dare she risk how others perceive me?" "What I came to realize," Natalie said, "was how much I actually care about what other people think of me even though on the outside, I never show that. It's been a big turning point for me to understand why I react the way I do in these situations."

A Reminder about Self-Compassion and Nonjudgment as You Spectate. As you can see in all the examples so far, building a spectating capability is not for the faint of heart. In fact, I don't usually introduce this concept to people who don't already have a strong baseline of self-awareness. It requires understanding that things can feel worse before they feel better. Many leaders are willing to take it on because they love the idea of continuous improvement. Others are just plain tired of situations where they know they're getting in their own way.

It's vital that you bring an attitude of nonjudgment and self-compassion to the endeavor of spectating your experience. You'll hinder your own efforts if you get caught up in self-blame, self-criticism, or self-pity. The irony is that our habit of being hard on ourselves is often the very thing we need to become aware of through self-spectating—and quite often, it's the thing most hindering us. Research has shown that when self-criticism runs rampant, it can lead to depression, anxiety, substance abuse, negative self-image, a preoccupation with failure, and decreased motivation and productivity. What's the remedy? Self-compassion. Multiple studies have shown that self-compassion—or being kind to oneself in the face of personal flaws or shortcomings—leads to greater achievement and personal improvement. Whereas self-criticism causes us to dwell on mistakes or shortcomings, self-compassion leads to clarity and self-acceptance that becomes the springboard for productive action.[9]

Step 2: Regulate: Find the Pause and Don't Scratch the Itch

Once you are clear on what is happening and why, you have a greater shot at not letting a trigger or emotion get the best of you. From here, the second step in the practice is to move from spectating to regulating.

Defuse the Emotional Charge. Part of why spectating and being able to see and accurately name what is happening is so effective is because it allows us to do what brain researchers call *cognitive labeling*, which has been shown to defuse some of the emotional charge that happens when we're triggered and in a Leader B mindset.[10] Labeling is just what it sounds like: we observe what's happening and then assign a label to it. Neuroscience researcher David Rock, who developed the SCARF model, says that cognitive labeling—which requires that you stop what you're doing and take the time to get an accurate read on a situation—is a far more effective technique than suppressing or denying an emotion. "The most successful executives have developed an ability to be in a state of high limbic system arousal and still remain calm," Rock writes. "Partly, this [comes from] their ability to label emotion states." His research shows that even using just one or two words can reduce the arousal of the brain's limbic system, which controls the fight-flight-freeze response, and activate the prefrontal cortex, which is responsible for executive functioning.[11] When you're in a crunch at work, for example, step back, observe your thoughts and your emotional state, and then put a label to what's happening, such as "stress," "high pressure," "overwhelmed," or "anxiety." It's a reliable way to get your brain back "online" after it's gone "off-line" due to emotional arousal.

Susan David, author of *Emotional Agility*, writes that dealing effectively with emotions is a critical skill for any leader, and the ability to name them is key. What's more, when people *don't* acknowledge and express their emotions, they're more likely to experience physical symptoms of stress (such as headaches), to suffer from anxiety or depressive disorders, and to resort to unhealthy coping mechanisms such as excessive drinking or aggression.[12] Tense, emotionally charged situations at work are bound to happen. The most effective leaders are able to defuse the emotional charge and retain their self-control.

Find the "Sacred Pause." As you become more skilled at noticing and naming your emotions, your body sensations, and the voice track in your mind, you will be able to hit the pause button more often. Not scratching the itch means we're not immediately reaching for a temporary form of relief and we're not reacting mindlessly. It means remaining grounded and being able to slow down enough to see our way to a more considered, productive response. One colleague described her learning process here as "noticing the initial feeling of discomfort, becoming fully aware of it, and taking a deep breath to bring things back to the frontal lobe." Chade-Meng Tan, author of *Search Inside Yourself* and creator of Google's renowned mindfulness-based emotional intelligence program of the same name, calls this moment a "sacred pause."[13]

The sacred pause is short but powerful—even just a few moments of not scratching the itch gives us a chance to determine how to move forward more effectively. Kris Nimsger, CEO of Social Solutions and formerly CEO of MicroEdge, and one of the most influential executives in the software industry today, once shared with me how she often mentors others in this area. Says Nimsger: "There is power in the pause between stimulus and response. The world is full of stimuli, and as we advance in our careers, the stimuli will only increase in its velocity and ferocity—period. Leaders need to function in a manner in which our behavior is not dictated by the stimulus but by the only thing we can actually control—which is our response."[14]

Increase Pause Time. We can build our ability to get better at finding and expanding that sacred pause by building greater emotional self-regulation. There are several ways to do this.

Use a mantra or swing thought. One of the easiest ways to find a sacred pause is to use a mantra or a swing thought.

A mantra is a sound, word, or phrase that one repeats, either aloud or silently in the mind, in order to gain focus and calm. The word *mantra* can be broken down into two parts: *man*, which means mind, and *tra*, which means transport or vehicle. Thus, a mantra is an instrument of the mind that's used to transport you to a state of calm, clarity, focus, and greater awareness.[15] The mantra itself isn't as important as the effect it produces, though sometimes people will choose words or phrases that convey their intention, such as "pause," "let go," or "one step at a time."

Some of my clients who are avid golfers call this a "swing thought"—a signal to cue the mind to settle down and re-anchor. If you practice your swing thought enough, it functions as an automatic "go" signal for your body to execute your swing without excess thought.[16] When a situation becomes tense or emotions are running high, a mantra or swing thought is a powerful signal to your mind and your body to return to a state of calm. And the more you use it, the more potent it becomes.

Sometimes, the cue to employ a mantra or swing thought is physical: Whenever Stefan, who was working on picking his battles, noticed his jaw clenching, he would say the mantra "not effective" to bring himself out of a heated reaction. Whenever Randy, who was working on delegation, noticed the pit in his stomach, he would say to himself, "Empower the team," as a reminder to step away from the keyboard and let go.

Use your breath. Mantras and swing thoughts approach emotional self-regulation through the mind. We can also increase our emotional control through the body. The easiest and most efficient—and for many people, the most effective—way to do this is through breathing. One of my favorite techniques is a type of yogic breathing I learned when I trained for my yoga teacher certification. This practice is called 4-7-8 breathing, and it's especially great for those who are short on time—it takes exactly one and a half minutes per day.

One of the best demonstrations of this practice comes from Dr. Andrew Weil, Harvard-trained physician and pioneer in the field of integrative medicine. Here's how it works:

- Inhale quietly through your nose for four seconds.

- Hold the breath for seven seconds.

- Exhale through the mouth for eight seconds.

- Repeat for four breath cycles.

Dr. Weil recommends practicing this technique twice a day, every day.[17] I've had clients report that 4-7-8 breathing helps them with insomnia (both getting to sleep and falling back asleep after waking in the night), prepresentation jitters, general anxiety, and getting present quickly.

Practice mindfulness meditation. In mindfulness meditation you are basically doing all the steps we've discussed so far—building your spectating muscle, finding the sacred pause, and not scratching the itch for a set amount of time.

Neuroscientist Amishi Jha, PhD, is doing pioneering work in the areas of mindfulness-based training, memory, and attention. She and her team have found that "the opposite of a stressed and wandering mind is a mindful one" and that the more we practice mindfulness— which she describes as "paying attention to our present moment experience with awareness and without any kind of emotional reactivity of what's happening"—the better we are at paying attention. And as with so many things, the more we practice mindfulness, the more we benefit. Participants who committed to doing a mindfulness practice on a daily basis for eight weeks not only retained their attention skills but improved them over time, even during high-stress situations such as an accountant during tax season or a student during final exams.[18]

There are many ways to practice mindfulness meditation; the key is to find the technique that suits you best. Here are some of the most popular. See which one resonates with you.

SITTING MEDITATION: The oldest-known form, sitting meditation, is what most people envision when they think of meditation. Whether you're in full lotus position on a zafu (a meditation cushion) or in a regular straight-back chair, this is the practice of sitting while you spectate and try not to scratch any itches (literally or figuratively!) for a specified length of time.

Within that definition there are endless ways to do it. Some are breath-based practices such as counting the cycles of inhalation and exhalation, simply bringing focused attention to the act of breathing, or engaging in a yogic breath practice such as the 4-7-8 I mentioned earlier. Others include focusing on an external object such as the flame of a candle or picking a point on the wall and staying focused there.

Most experts recommend sitting at least twenty minutes because it takes us that long to calm down and settle in, but if you're new to meditation, start with a shorter span of time and work your way up. Give yourself credit for *any* amount of time you devote to stepping out of the fray and practicing your spectating ability.

You can also use technology to support your practice. Several apps offer guided meditation, and many people find it's easier to put on headphones and make the most of white-space time (from chapter 3) that way. Rich Fernandez, the CEO of the Search Inside Yourself Leadership Institute, a nonprofit organization developed at Google, recommends the meditation apps Calm, Headspace, and Muse.[19] I'm personally a fan of Insight Timer, which offers a mix of guided meditations, calming music, and a timer for those who prefer silence.

WALKING MEDITATION: For those of you who want to pick up meditation but find that sitting just isn't working, I'd recommend you try walking meditation. Many of the leaders I work with are too busy for an extended "sit" or find it too difficult to settle down enough, and have found they are able to stick to this practice more easily.

Give this a try:

- Pick the area where you will do your walking meditation. It could be the length of a hallway or the length of your street.

- Walk the length of the set area without judgment.

- Walk at a similar pace back and forth for a specified amount of time—like sitting meditation, twenty minutes is usually a good length for settling in.

- As you walk, notice where your attention is, where it drifts, and keep bringing your attention back to the action of walking.

Jack Kornfield, PhD, a world-renowned mindfulness teacher, has likened walking meditation—and our ever-wandering mind—to training a puppy. "You will need to come back a thousand times," he says. "Whether you have been away for one second or for ten minutes, no matter. Simply acknowledge where you have been and then come back to being alive here and now with the next step you take."[20]

I was recently with a group of executives for a retreat held off-site at a resort. As part of our discussion around how we could continue to expand our impact and influence with less stress and more presence, I asked them to do an experiment with me and try out walking meditation.

I picked out a spot in the courtyard purposefully as it included high traffic, and I wanted to raise everyone's self-consciousness level and make it hard to keep their attention on the act of walking. For a full ten minutes, I asked the executives to walk the length of the courtyard, keeping a steady pace, and to simply notice and spectate.

When we came back inside, I asked the group how many of them thought I had gone crazy and were thinking, "What are we doing? This is ridiculous!" Just about every hand in the room shot up.

Then, I asked them to describe the experience. One CFO raised her hand and shared, "At first, I *did* think this was a crazy exercise, and I really didn't want to do it. Especially when other people passed by us, I noticed how embarrassed and self-conscious I felt and how resentful I was that we were doing this at all.

"But at some point, I found that for the first time since being here, I was noticing the sound of the water coming from the main fountain and just what a beautiful place this is. I realized I hadn't even noticed there was a fountain until then. It was actually pretty incredible how present and engaged I felt by the time the ten minutes was up."

CLEAN-UP MEDITATION: This is a mindfulness meditation practice I've devised on my own. I've found it to be one of the most effective ways for me to really learn to pay attention and be fully present in my mind and in my body, and be less reactive. The idea struck me when I read an article in an airline magazine that covered how lots of Silicon Valley types were all flying to an ashram in California to learn meditation. But instead of sitting around meditating all day, a good portion of their days was spent sweeping and cleaning.

One of the concepts in Zen that I've long been fascinated by is engaging with a task or with a person with one's whole self. What does it mean to engage with zeal, without distraction, and with full presence? Imagine a day where the amount of effort and energy you expend is exactly the right amount required for the situation at hand. Contrast that with the energy we burn when we're in a state of high reactivity, self-sabotage, or acute stress.

On the surface, this quintessential Zen practice sounds very simple: "When doing dishes, just do the dishes." "When sweeping the floor, just sweep the floor." But as I've experimented with that in my own life, the truth is that even the simple task of trying to wash the dishes with full focus and engaged attention is far easier said than done. Think back to the last time you cleaned up after dinner and did the dishes. How often did your mind wander off with all kinds of thoughts and judgments? "I can't believe I have to do so many dishes! I have to remember to send that email to the team tonight. I am so annoyed there are so many dishes to do. I can't believe how behind I am on that deliverable. What will I cook for dinner tomorrow?" As each thought emerges, consider the corresponding physiological reactions. The next thing you know, you're stressed and overwhelmed by all that's running through your mind instead of just washing the dishes.

But like the puppy who always wanders off and needs gentle guidance back, just continue to bring your mind back to washing the dishes the first moment you notice you've gone wandering. Maintain an attitude of nonjudgment: the puppy is just acting according to his nature, after all, and needs training. So it is with our minds, and the more we train, the better we get.

Ultimately, it doesn't matter what type of mindfulness meditation practice you choose. The intent is the same: to carve out some time for yourself and to practice spectating, coming back to yourself without judgment and getting present over and over again, and not scratching the itch. The application and benefits then extend into your daily life: when you're engaged in *any* task or situation, you'll find that you are more quickly able to get present, engaged, and effective, whether you're leading a meeting, collaborating with your team, sending a thoughtful email, or spending time with family and friends.

Step 3: Adapt: Realize the Power of Choice and Create New If-Thens

A more constructive set of choices emerges when we see and experience the present moment with less reaction—even while, with full awareness, experiencing anxiety, fear, anger, sadness, or other uncomfortables emotions, rather than unconsciously letting them drive us. When we realize there is choice—between Leader A and Leader B mode—we move through all steps of this practice: from spectating to regulating to adapting. It takes time, courage, self-compassion, and willingness to come to the junctures in the road over and over again where we realize we are ready for the next best version of ourselves.

Recognize New Choices. One of the toughest patterns I struggle with is responding to stress with my temporary fix of choice, sugar.

When stressed or anxious—or on the other end of the spectrum, after a major win or deliverable—I reach for sugar. It's a vicious cycle: I reach for candy, ice cream, soda, you name it. Internally, my voice track is all about entitlement: "I deserve this pleasure. I deserve this candy bar. I deserve this bowl of chocolate ice cream." That's all fine and good, except that my family is filled with diabetics, and sugar brings out the worst in me. When it's coursing through my body, it impacts my presence and my effectiveness. For me, the effects are worse than missing out on sleep or exercise.

I know this, and while I haven't fully cut sugar from my diet, I am choosing sugar less often, and I do find that I am getting better at getting back on track with more ease and less self-criticism. While I'm not even close to batting 1,000, part of what has made getting back on track just a little easier has been changing my mindset and recognizing the power of choice.

Rather than it being a reward for a job well done or a tempting form of self-soothing, I now recognize that sugar is an important cue that alerts me I am standing at the fork in the road between Leader A and Leader B. For me, sugar signals that something is awry—that there is something I'm not attending to, something I'm not asking for, or something I'm not feeling acknowledged for. When I'm at my best, I adapt by reaching for a pen and paper or other people instead of candy:

- How can I write out what's bothering me rather than eating my way to okay-ness?

- Which of my safe harbors and cheerleaders can I reach out to (chapter 4) to ask for help?

- Do I need to reshuffle or reprioritize or renegotiate a deadline (chapter 2)?

This method isn't perfect, and it doesn't mean I don't enjoy dessert after a great meal. But given the genetics in my family and the impact sugar has on my overall effectiveness, I know that healthier coping mechanisms are important to being the leader I want to be. I'm especially mindful of my sugar intake during weeks when I have high-stakes situations or events where being at my best and most effective is critical.

It is no surprise that our physical well-being is directly interconnected with our ability to be more present and less reactive. Everyone knows that it's easier to be your highest and best self after a good night's sleep, eating well, or getting some exercise. Rather than have any of those things become a "should," we can use spectating and an expanded awareness to understand exactly which lever most directly impacts effectiveness and then put some choice around the whole thing.

Rather than going cold turkey or holding yourself to some expectation that only sets you up for self-criticism, choose to limit caffeine, sugar, or alcohol, especially when you need to be fully sharp and present. Choose to get that one really great night of sleep before a big presentation, or get in a run during the change effort you are leading at work, when the stress may be especially high. Part of feeding Leader A is knowing which situations require you to be especially present and effective, and recognizing the plethora of choices you can make to meet those moments.

Create New If-Thens. One of the most effective ways to create new patterns is to use a research-proven technique known as the *if-then* tool. This is a simple mental framework used to set up a new process or healthy habit, meet a goal, or increase our overall presence. When your spectating self detects a trigger, you can use the if-then framework to create better ways to respond.

A leader, Julianne, used the if-then framework to gain clarity on her old patterns and create a new one that led her to choose a way to remain present rather than become reactive. Here's how she did it:

- OLD PATTERN: "If triggered by an annoying colleague, then I respond by ruminating about it and wasting time and energy having imaginary conversations with that person in my head."

- NEW PATTERN: "If triggered by an annoying colleague, then I will leave my desk and do five minutes of 4-7-8 breathing to figure out if this is a battle worth fighting or something to let go."

EXERCISE

The If-Then Tool

Give this a try yourself. Think of an old pattern that you know no longer works for you—one that impedes your effectiveness or your ability to reach a goal you want to achieve.

Write down first the old if-then pattern:

- **Old pattern:** If triggered by _____, then I have historically responded by _____.

Now, write down the new pathway you'd like to create:

- **New pattern:** If triggered by _____, then I will now
  _____.

If-then plans work because our brains are very good at encoding information in "If x, then y" terms and using those connections (often unconsciously) to guide behavior. In this way they function much like a mantra. It seems that when we decide exactly when, where, and how to fulfill our goals, our brains create a neurological link between a situation or cue ("If or when x happens") and the behavior that should follow ("then I will do y"). Research bears this out. Based on more than two hundred studies, researchers have found that if-then planners are about 300 percent more likely than others to reach their goals. Once the brain detects an "if," it automatically triggers a "then." (For example, "If it's 2 p.m. on Friday, then I will submit my report.") In this way the brain triggers action *without you having to think about it.*[21] You're setting up an ingrained mental cue that eliminates any mental effort involved in figuring out what to do and how to do it. You're left with the luxury of getting straight to the task at hand.

Peter Gollwitzer, the psychologist who first studied if-then planning, has described this powerful if-then mechanism as creating "instant habits," the kind that help you reach your goals. Studies show that whether we're trying to complete work projects, save for retirement, obtain preventive health care, or lose weight, despite our best intentions, we fail to follow through roughly 50 percent of the time. Why? Sometimes we don't act because we're too busy to notice opportunities to do so. Sometimes we lose confidence in our ability to achieve a goal, so we push it to a mental back burner, like Yasmina did. Or we just let competing goals, motivations, or temptations bubble up to the top of the priority list. This is where if-then planning can preclude some of those common roadblocks to achieving a goal and help us follow through when problems arise.

Have Greater Choice in Voice. We'll end this chapter by looking at how presence helps us to show up more often as Leader A in how we communicate. When we have greater access to all the parts of ourselves and more emotional self-control, we also gain a greater *choice of voice*. By staying present fully no matter the situation at hand, we can engage in what Buddhists call "right speech and right action."

You Don't Need Just One Leadership Voice, You Need Many

We often equate developing a leadership voice with finding ways to appear more confident. We assume that our success depends on mimicking someone else, promoting ourselves, or saying things louder than others. You can build true confidence by more intentionally focusing on cultivating different voices. Ultimately, you should cultivate enough parts of your voice so that no matter the leadership situation or audience you find yourself facing, you can respond in an authentic, constructive, and effective way. So, what are the various voices to access within yourself and cultivate over time? And what are the situations that warrant each voice?

Your Voice of Character

First and foremost, consider the voice of your character. This is the part of your voice that is constant and consistent. It is grounded in fundamental principles about whom you choose to be and about what guides and motivates your interactions with others. I've had leaders share that, like a mantra, they hold key leadership principles in mind such as "Give the benefit of the doubt," "Don't take things personally," "Focus on what's best for the business," or "Be direct with respect" when walking into a difficult conversation or meeting or a potential conflict. Anchoring ourselves in the character we know we have keeps us from becoming chameleons, acting out of a fight-or-flight reaction, or showing respect only when there is a commercial gain or benefit. A voice of character is ultimately about who you are at your core and the intentions and motivations that guide your speech and actions. The more you cultivate presence, the more you use your voice of character.

Your Voice of Context

As you take on increasingly senior roles, your perspective of the business grows. You hold more of the big picture. Part of the job then becomes finding ways to express and communicate that bigger picture to others. Too often, in the race against time, we dive right into the details of a presentation, meeting, or conversation without taking an extra few minutes to appropriately set the stage and share critical context.

Situations where you can bring more of your voice of context include:

- Sharing vision, strategy, or upcoming organizational change with others

- Presenting to executives, and being clear on what you are there for and what you need

- Kicking off a meeting with your team and giving the larger context for the topic at hand

- Making your decision-making criteria or rationale transparent to others

Your Voice of Clarity

In a world of high-intensity workplaces, you have the opportunity to be the voice of clarity and help your team stay focused on the most important priorities. Leaders who end up in the I'll Just Do It Now Pitfall reflexively fire off new possibilities, muse out loud, or have knee-jerk reactions, running the risk of teams trying to deliver on their every whim. These teams end up scattered, spread thin, and unfocused, falling short on delivering the most important wins. Relying on your spectator self automatically precludes much of this type of mindless, reactive behavior, but here are a few more ways you can be the voice of clarity to help channel others' energies more productively:

- At the start of the year, sit down with each direct report to prioritize and clarify what the big wins are in each of their areas. One client shared how she asks each team member: "If we were to publish this in a newspaper, what would you want the big headlines to be for you and your team at the end of the year?"

- Periodically come back to helping your direct reports reprioritize what's on their plates. You can do this in one-on-one meetings or with your entire team.

- Empower your team to say no.

Your Voice of Curiosity

As a leader, you have a responsibility to give direction, share information, and make important decisions. But you need to be sure that you're not approaching every situation as if you have all the answers or as if you need to advise on, problem-solve, or fix everything in front of you. In many cases, being the voice of curiosity is a better choice for the situation. As one of my clients once shared about facing pushback from others, "While I'm confident in my own business judgment and instincts, I know that my organization has hired really smart people. Therefore, if one of my peers or team members has a different perspective or pushes back, I don't take it personally. I get really curious to understand where they are coming from first so that we can get to the best solution." Some situations where bringing your voice of curiosity can help you and your colleagues move forward include:

- When you're engaging in work that is interdependent, and a better solution will come from hearing all perspectives in the room before coming to a final decision

- When you're coaching a direct report and asking good questions to help them grow in new ways, explore issues they're facing, or support their career development

- When you're in a difficult conversation where hearing out the other person is an important part of defusing emotion, understanding each party's needs and views, and then figuring out the best way forward

Your Voice of Connection

As your span of control or influence grows, it can become increasingly difficult to make a connection with a broadening set of colleagues, strategic networks, and teams. It's not uncommon to have people working for us many layers deep into the organization, such that we no longer know everyone in our area and still must find ways to stay connected and visible. Being a voice of connection can come in many forms. Here are some of the ways I've seen leaders do this effectively:

- INCREASE YOUR SKILL AS A STORYTELLER: Stories make our points more memorable and salient. They can enliven a keynote address or an all-hands meeting, drive home a point we're making in a presentation, or help to close a large deal or transaction.

- THANK AND ACKNOWLEDGE: Our teams and colleagues often go to great lengths to ensure that deliverables are met, revenues are strong, and customers are satisfied. When we use our voice of connection, we remember to express gratitude to a team that worked through the holidays to close on the financials at the end of the quarter, or we remember to loop back to a colleague who made a valuable introduction or referral for us.

- MAKE TIME FOR A FEW MINUTES OF ICE-BREAKING OR RAPPORT-BUILDING AT THE START OF A CONVERSATION OR MEETING: So often, we want to get right down to business, so we skip the niceties or pleasantries that help to build relationships with others. Where possible, and especially with colleagues who value that kind of connection, spend a couple of minutes to connect before diving into the work. On days where you're crunched for time, state that up front and transparently, so as not to create any misunderstandings. You can say something like: "I'm a little crunched for time today, so it would be great if we could dive right in."

Discovering and developing your voice as a leader is the work of a lifetime. It is a huge part of increasing the fourth P, presence, and in accessing your authentic self. The key is to use each situation as an opportunity to access more parts of your voice rather than having a one-size-fits-all approach. Bring your voices of character, context, clarity, curiosity, and connection as the moment or situation warrants. Through this kind of learning and growth, not only will you increase your inner confidence and resilience, but you will also inspire the confidence of others around you in a more authentic and meaningful way.

Expand Your Leadership Voice

Increasing your ability to influence and communicate more effectively with others requires that you take a look at your leadership voice today. Answer the following questions and see where you have specific opportunity to grow in your "choice of voice":

1. Which leadership voice comes most naturally to you?

2. Which leadership voice do you lose access to, or perhaps comes less naturally to you, when you are triggered or under stress?

3. Which voice could you further develop and cultivate to be more effective in your job?

The Fully Present Leader

We've all worked with colleagues or bosses who seem to be there "in body only." They're distracted or lack concentration, or they appear to be a million miles away. Not being present is a hallmark sign of being in Leader B mode, where old patterns of fear, stress, insecurity, or anxiety run the show.

Leaders who display the fourth P, presence, embody the opposite qualities. From the inside, we feel grounded, centered, and calm. When we listen, we listen with our full attention, not scanning a mental to-do list or planning what we're going to say next. From the outside, we come across as fully engaged, attending to the moment at hand with attention and without distraction. When we've cultivated presence, we have greater access to our best selves, and we're able to respond thoughtfully rather than impulsively. We don't take things as personally, and we're able to hold a larger perspective. From this place, we are more likely to take on greater roles and responsibilities and know that we'll meet the moment as Leader A no matter what is thrown our way.

What to Remember:

➤ We've all had times when it feels like we aren't progressing or aren't present to the areas of our lives that are the most important to us. It's not unusual to have times when we just can't help ourselves and we want to scratch the itch. Rather than being present and making choices in service of our effectiveness or next-level impact, we instead get trapped and self-sabotage by engaging in old patterns, or we fall into habits of distraction, perfectionism, procrastination, or rumination.

➤ Presence helps us to keep our focus and attention to move forward important goals, increases our emotional resilience to tolerate what may be uncomfortable in the short term to learn new patterns and practices that create and sustain long-term progress, and builds our inner capacity to pause between stimulus and response to make more thoughtful, wise decisions. When we have the capacity to be aware and grounded in the here and now and are able to exert our full attention, we make the leadership choice based on what's best for the moment.

➤ You can get present quickly so that distraction or procrastination don't get the better of you by (1) choosing to work off-line, (2) bringing your focus from the mountain to the molehill and taking single steps, (3) giving yourself fifteen minutes to get into a flow, (4) staying anchored in the physical, or (5) using a grounding visualization technique to quickly bring attention and focus to the present moment.

➤ You can shift to more virtuous, positive cycles by using the practice of (1) spectating and observing the patterns at play, (2) finding and extending the "pause" time between stimulus and response through greater self-regulation, and (3) adapting by creating new if-then patterns and choosing the best leadership action or voice for the situation at hand. This helps to break reactive patterns or vicious cycles that burn up energy, waste time, and lead to ineffectiveness and dissatisfaction.

➤ With more control and choice over our emotional states, we gain greater access to all parts of our authentic self and increase our overall *choice of voice*. The five leadership voices include voice of character, voice of context, voice of clarity, voice of curiosity, and voice of connection. You can tap into the leadership voice needed to maintain presence and meet the leadership challenge at hand.

CHAPTER SIX

The Power of Peace

Loosen Your Grip

M ark stood out in my mind because he was one of those people who seemed to move from win to win. Remarkably intelligent and motivated, he graduated from a top university and graduate program and, to no one's surprise, landed a job at a large investment bank right out of school. His early career was marked by a succession of promotions, and as he moved into midcareer, he transitioned seamlessly back into industry and soon after earned the coveted CFO position at his company. He'd sought out coaching to help navigate this huge jump in responsibility and all the pressures associated with it. He approached our work together with the same fervor and dedication he applied to any endeavor, and I remember feeling as if I learned as much from Mark as he did from me.

Two years later, he was back for more coaching. I asked Mark to give me a rundown of the past couple of years since he'd taken on such a vastly expanded role. I learned that the past year had been particularly incredible, and just one week prior, he'd received a stellar performance review. In fact, not only had it been his best year ever in terms of performance, but he felt his most energetic, enthusiastic, and healthy as well. I knew from our previous work together that Mark had a well-developed spectator capability and was generally present to himself and what was happening. So I was quite curious to hear what had prompted him to return to coaching now.

Mark explained that he was worried about a mental dynamic he was noticing. Though he had clearly gained greater success and influence, not to mention financial and professional security, he couldn't shake the feeling that something was still missing. He described feeling "unsettled and dissatisfied" in a way he couldn't quite put his finger on.

It seemed that each time Mark thought he'd met a career-making deliverable or received a big promotion or professional accolade, he'd have a sense of completion and satisfaction—but it never remained. Before he knew it, he was looking to the next big deliverable and the next promotion, and the cycle would begin again. Mark had now been through this cycle enough times that he was aware of the pattern. As we talked about what was changing—why all these successes no longer felt like enough—several things emerged. On the home front, Mark's kids would be leaving for college in a few years, and he was worried about spending enough time with them. Meanwhile, his mother was having health problems, and the reality of having aging parents was sinking in. Professionally, despite his many successes and, as he put it, "a life where I could hardly hope for more," he was troubled by his lack of interior peace. "I guess I always thought when I got to this stage of my career, to this point in life, that I'd have a sense of satisfaction. Some kind of deeper feeling like all this was *enough*." Why, he wondered, were moments of feeling like Leader A so fleeting—especially when he had earned every external marker of success?

Mark said he could feel himself standing at a critical juncture. He loved his work and felt as ambitious as ever but shared that he often felt he was "living in between here and now," trying to be present but finding himself anxious about the future. He confessed that he didn't know if he could keep this up for the next twenty years. He wanted to understand how he could cultivate the ability to live—at work and at home—with more peace and a sense of satisfaction and meaning. "If I'm going to work this hard," he concluded, "I want to be able to enjoy the ride along the way *and* trust that what I'm doing has some kind of greater worth."

The Connection between Peace and Being Leader A or Leader B

Mark is not unlike many of us who have achieved a certain level of success and yet remain troubled by a kind of low-simmering worry that prevents us from feeling fully satisfied. It's as if we just can't relax or give ourselves permission to pause and enjoy our success for fear that if we ease up a little, everything we've worked so hard to build will crumble. Wanting to protect what we've built is normal, as is the desire to continue growing and improving. But leaders can find themselves in Leader B mode when they get stuck, as if on a hamster wheel, continuously striving and trying to prove themselves. If we don't loosen the grip we hold on ourselves and accept and trust in who we are and what we have, there's no chance, as Mark put it, to enjoy the ride along the way.

In this chapter, we'll look at our final P, peace, which is about coming to a place of acceptance and equanimity. Rather than approach peace as some abstract concept, I'll first share with you three concrete ways to live and lead with more peace and less stress and worry. We'll then discuss how from a foundation of greater peace, you can be released from the exhaustion that comes from a state of constant striving to a more effortless and fulfilling state of greater intrinsic motivation and purpose.

If we can be sure our leadership actions stem less from a need to prove, self-preserve, or one-up others (or ourselves, as in Mark's case), we open the door to a realm of greater meaning, fulfillment, and transformation on both the personal and the organizational level. And in the end, we end up coming full circle to our first P, purpose, where concepts like servant leadership and paying it forward become part of being Leader A.

"ACT" with Peace

As leaders have privately shared their worries, frustrations, and moments of doubt, I've created an easy acronym as a reminder for the ways you can access more peace and satisfaction.

"ACT" stands for the following:

- A = ACCEPT THE MOMENT: Take constructive and effective action for what's within your control.

- C = BE CONTENT IN THE MOMENT: Know what's enough and bring an attitude of gratitude.

- T = TRUST YOURSELF AND LIFE IN THE MOMENT: You've achieved, learned, and grown, and you will do so again.

#1: *Accept* the Moment

The first letter of A in ACT stands for acceptance. A first step toward greater peace is seeing and accepting that life and leadership will *always* contain a range of seemingly opposing experiences. Life can bring happiness, joy, learning, growth, and achievement, and it will also bring its fair share of sorrow, grief, pain, hurt, anger, and sadness. Even things your mind deems as positive—such as getting a promotion, closing an acquisition, or making that lucrative sale—can just as easily bring feelings of stress and vulnerability. All new things bring both a level of joy and a level of uncertainty.

Name the Resistance: What Don't You Accept? Part of cultivating a best self includes being able to ride the wave and stay in flow even amid that mix of experiences and emotions. This requires increasing your capability to manage resistance within yourself. Resistance may be a good sign to pay attention, or it can be a cue to trust your intuition that something is wrong. However, know the point of diminishing returns with resistance—when good worry becomes rumination or becomes unproductive.

Taken to the extreme, the instinct to run from what feels adverse can burn up a lot of unnecessary and unproductive time and energy. When we continually avoid and resist what we should be paying attention to, we stall out or even regress. Especially when we're faced with the unknown or hit a setback, it can be easy to fall into the downside of resistance. This kind of resistance usually looks and feels like this:

- In your mind: I WISH THIS WEREN'T HAPPENING.

- In your heart: I WANT AND EXPECT SOMETHING ELSE.

- In your body: I'M SO TENSE (OR IN PAIN, OR TIRED).

Physicists define resistance as "the degree to which a substance or device opposes the passage of an electric current, causing energy dissipation."[1] The greater the degree of resistance, the more energy is lost. Think about that in terms of your development as a leader—*the more you resist or oppose what's happening, the more energy you lose.* How often do you experience resistance and the subsequent energy drain that comes with it? See if you've found yourself experiencing any of the following forms of resistance in the past month:

- You miss "the good ol' days" and want things to be like they were before the company reorganized.

- You can't stand the things you have to work on while you're in the process of making a key hire.

- You wish the colleague who annoys you most would change their ways or just resign.

- You really wish that someone could give you reassurance that you'll get promoted.

- You hate that you caught a terrible cold right at the worst time during the quarter.

- You are resentful that you had to leave behind the more leisurely pace you had during vacation.

- You feel jealous that your classmate from business school makes more money than you do.

- You look at pictures of yourself from another time, annoyed that you are not as fit as you once were.

All these feelings are entirely natural. But when you're caught up in resistance, you're not present to what is happening right in front of you. You're wasting a lot of energy in feeding your resistance and feeding Leader B—which keeps you from addressing the issue that's bothering you.

What's the opposite of resistance? If we turn back to physics for just a moment, we find that resistance's opposite is conductance. Conductance is "the ease with which an electric current passes" through a conductor; a conductor is a substance through which electricity flows.[2] Let's again think about this in leadership terms. If you're not resisting—if you're accepting—you're *gaining* energy and allowing energy to flow. Therefore, for greater "leadership conductance" and flow, acceptance is the doorway to gaining energy and change.

Be Honest: What's in Your Control? What Is Out of Your Control? Acceptance is *not* giving in, giving up, or being passive. In fact, acceptance is all about being honest and facing your situation head-on so you can take constructive action. When you are in Leader A mode, you are more quickly able to separate what is out of your control (e.g., "I can't change that annoying colleague's personality," or "I can't stop the reorg from happening") from what is within your control (e.g., "I am going to have more difficult conversations," or "I'm going to more proactively figure out how I fit into this new structure"). Once you're clear on what you can't control, you can stop wasting time and energy ruminating about it.

All of this awareness requires a certain level of wisdom and discernment, and that requires that we allow ourselves to fully see and own up to what's happening, even if it's a situation we don't like or that doesn't feel good. Remember that one of the chief values of self-spectating is to see reality as it really is, to be fully aware of the present moment, in whatever form it arrives. As my son's volleyball coach tells the team, "Sometimes you have to embrace the suck."

"Embrace the suck" is a wonderful mantra from Brené Brown's book, *Dare to Lead*, and the coach uses it to help the team when they have to get up early for tournaments and are tired and hungry and generally unhappy.[3] But it's a good mantra for anyone who is struggling with acceptance. I've certainly used it to help me get through some difficult weeks of travel and intense work.

Let's say you really don't like that extra fifteen pounds you put on. What's the first step in doing something about it? Acceptance. Without acceptance, you stay stuck in either attachment to the past (when you weighed less) or somewhere in an imagined future (when you will weigh less). Acceptance brings us to a more truthful, open state. It's only from there that we can take purposeful, helpful action rather than avoid a situation or take a toxic or negative action. This applies to anything in life, whether it's losing that stubborn fifteen pounds, making a clear and direct request of our annoying colleague, more proactively finding opportunities in the reorg, or just getting into bed to get over that cold more quickly.

If you find that your resistance runs especially deep, then a lack of acceptance may be the issue. One leader, after weeks of self-spectating and writing down her observations, noticed a pattern: any time she found herself "endlessly complaining," it was a cue that she was in a state of high resistance. As she continued spectating and became more present to the moment, she noted that the weeks she had virtually no white space on her calendar and an overflowing inbox made her feel "nagged and bombarded from all sides," which in turn left her irritable and frazzled and far more apt to complain. This leader learned to accept that an empty inbox wasn't realistic—and that neither was it realistic that *all* those meetings she was saying yes to tapped into her highest and best use. She realized she'd drifted off into extremes—*I want an empty inbox; it's imperative that I attend every meeting*—and that accepting the reality of the situation and aiming more for the middle way was her path to far greater peace and less resistance.

Let Go to Accept. Letting go of old patterns and areas of resistance can sometimes happen in an "aha moment," especially for everyday matters such as resistance to working on that expense report, to coming back from vacation, or to our email inboxes piling up. In cases like these, just being able to recognize that the expectation to have an empty inbox is not reasonable, for example, especially during a busy season, can ease the resistance.

But we all have areas of resistance that are deeply embedded, such as an attachment to an idealized image of ourselves, or the expectation of how we want something to turn out. When resistance is strong, coming to acceptance and being present is a much slower process, and sometimes, frankly, it's never-ending work.

When we find ourselves in a transition or change, we often go through several stages that can look like this:

FIGURE 6-1

Stages of transitions and change

Resistance → Anger → Grief → Letting go → Acceptance → New beginnings

When you look at the stages noted here, you can see there's a process involved in moving from resistance to acceptance, and ultimately to a new way of being. I don't think we can sugarcoat or be naïve about the work and time that's required when we're not at peace and when resistance is getting in the way of taking on larger roles or of being effective, present, or satisfied. Getting to acceptance often means having to get real with yourself and experience difficult emotions such as anger or resentment, or the underlying sadness, grief, or vulnerability that comes with it.

I know for me personally, one of the hardest things I've had to come to peace with is being a full-time working parent. On my Leader B days, my lens is cloudy, and I feel resistant and resentful. I see work and my family as an "either-or" problem, as competing commitments rather than parts of myself that compose a larger whole. I end up annoyed that I'm on the road or frustrated that I'm working late again, or guilty and sad that I'm missing out on being with my son. The inner critic in my head is louder than ever, and I end up wasting a lot of energy resisting the fact that I'm in a busy period. Left unchecked, I telegraph the repressed and denied emotions as stress to my team, bring a subpar self to clients, or, ironically enough, am distracted and not present when I finally get to be with my family.

I recently read a *Time* magazine profile on Serena Williams that powerfully and poignantly captured the pull between the desire to be our highest and best as a professional and our highest and best as a parent. No stranger to the limelight, Serena found herself the subject of a different sort of media coverage after getting back to the courts following a birth that brought life-threatening complications, multiple surgeries, and a difficult recovery. While the world marveled over her extraordinary athletic ability, Serena agonized over missing out on time with her infant daughter while she trained. What carried her through the low moments, she said, was knowing moms around the world were rallying around her. She dedicated her return to Wimbledon, where she made it to the finals, "to all the moms out there who've been through a lot." Which didn't necessarily make it any easier: "Some days, I cry," she said. "Some days I'm really sad. I've had meltdowns. It's been a really tough 11 months. If I can do it, you guys can do it too."[4]

Even for Serena Williams, who is at the top of her profession and whose success has afforded her ample resources, including help with childcare, finding balance between being a full-time professional athlete and a parent is a struggle. Even Serena Williams must make the conscious effort to be present and see the moment for what it is, and then make a choice to act from a Leader A mindset. Sometimes that means hitting the gym, sometimes that means protecting her processes so she can perform at her best, and sometimes that means adhering to a strict time limit on her workouts so she can protect time with her daughter. Like all of us, she's learning as she goes and making decisions in the moment. "Nothing about me right now is perfect," she said. "But I'm perfectly Serena."[5]

Some areas of acceptance are easier to get to than others. They all need to be handled with self-compassion and self-care, and when we find that our resistance is running especially deep, part of living out of Leader A mode is knowing when we need to reach out for help—and having the courage to do it.

EXERCISE

Leadership Conductance—Move from Resistance to Action

Often, we feel frustrated or drained but are not fully aware of what the underlying resistance may be. It's important to periodically check in to see where it is in your life you want something to be different from what it is now:

1. Where in your work or home life do you currently experience a high level of frustration, drain, or resistance?

2. What does your mind say about it? Your heart? Your body?

3. What is within your control about the situation?

4. What is out of your control? What do you need to accept about the situation?

5. What is a constructive action you can take on what is within your control at this time?

Own and Embrace All Parts of Yourself. The A in ACT is also about accepting all the parts of ourselves and the full range of our experiences.

There are parts of ourselves we feel pride in and that define our leadership identity: "I'm a good person. I'm a strong person. I'm a visionary. I have a huge capacity for work and tons of grit. I achieve many great things. I'm a fun, optimistic person. I can see across the horizon faster than others can."

Likewise, there will always be parts of ourselves we wish we could tuck away and ignore: "I'm overly ambitious. I can be petty. I feel overwhelmed. I am vulnerable. I'm impatient. I do need others. I naturally worry a lot."

For Mark, coming to greater peace meant that he needed to come to accept and integrate the parts of himself that didn't feel like his idea of a leader. He didn't like the times he felt overwhelmed, unsettled, or "not at peace." These experiences made him feel vulnerable, which didn't square with the image of the strong, decisive, visionary leader he prided himself to be.

But as Mark became more willing to be present to his feelings of worry and vulnerability, he realized there was actually a positive side to *some* of his angst and that spending so much time and energy resisting it was doing himself a disservice. On the upside, his angst kept him humble, kept him on his toes, and pushed him always to reach for excellence and high quality. His worry propelled him to dig a little deeper to get to the best outcome and solution. Mark was naturally a creative and visionary person, so he came to see that part of his process would always bring with it some amount of "inner artistic turmoil." He'd always felt a degree of anxiety when he was on a new learning curve or in a new situation—but he realized that every time, he got up and over that curve.

As Mark came to see and make peace with the unpeaceful parts of himself, he started to accept this part of his experience with less resistance. This new self-acceptance did not mean complacency. He was always going to be someone who wanted to get better and grow. But self-acceptance did help Mark release himself from the pressure to uphold some idealized image of a mythical "superman," and to more compassionately see he was both an excellent leader and also a leader who could still improve. With this vision in place, he could begin letting go of the judgment of the parts of himself he didn't like and direct his energy toward improving.

Acceptance doesn't mean we resign ourselves to a negative situation or give up on an area that needs improvement. Acceptance is ultimately about truth-seeking—the way you might conduct diligence for an acquisition or when trying to get to the best answer on a business problem. Only when we accept the truth of a situation can we take any meaningful action.

#2: Be *Content* in the Moment

The C in ACT stands for contentment. Before we delve deep into contentment, let's first look at its flip side, dissatisfaction. There's a lot of talk about attaining satisfaction in your life and in your

WIDENING THE LEADER A LENS: SEEING PARTS OF A WHOLE RATHER THAN OPPOSITES

Much of this chapter is ultimately about cultivating a greater internal balance. The challenges leaders face often pull us to extremes, and our brains want to move to the extreme that brings us the most comfort, which is not necessarily what's best for the business, organization, or situation at hand.

Like every leader, you will face managing for short-term profit results and long-term growth; speed to task and decision and collaborative process; holding the bigger picture and being in the detail; and dealing with your agenda and the agenda of another person or function.

But rather than bringing a narrow lens that only sees each of these tensions as an either-or situation, you can widen the lens to see that these things are vital parts of a greater whole.

One term that captures this state of internal balance is *equanimity*. Equanimity has Latin roots that literally mean "even mind." The *Oxford English Dictionary* describes equanimity as fairness of judgment, evenness of mind or temper, and being undisturbed by any "agitating emotion."[a] It's one of the pinnacle characteristics and experiences of the Leader A mindset, and it comes directly from a well-developed spectator ability and the practice of regularly and mindfully aligning yourself to the five Ps.

As you become more skilled at accessing your inner spectator and leading from a place of peace and equanimity, you are eventually more able to live in what some call the *middle way*. In Buddhism, the middle way is found "between the extremes of indulgence and self-denial," and it is identified as "the way to peace and liberation in this very life."[b] Likewise, Western thought, going all the way back to the ancient Greeks, advises us to aim for the *golden mean*, which Aristotle describes as "the desirable middle between two extremes."[c]

Following this desirable middle path does not mean watering down or compromising; it means you are no longer pulled by opposing forces. You are neither too reactionary nor too passive; you instead see objectively and clearly what is in front of you, and you choose not what restrains or indulges but what is the effective, constructive, and right thing to do. Learning to rest in the middle way, says Jack Kornfield, author and one of the key teachers to introduce Buddhist mindfulness practice to the West, means "we neither remove ourselves from the world nor get lost in it. We can be with all our experience in its complexity, with our own exact thoughts and feelings and drama as it is. We learn to embrace tension, paradox, change. Instead of seeking resolution . . . we let ourselves open and relax in the middle."[d]

When we are no longer at the mercy of being pulled by the extremes, our Leader A perspective widens and grows. We're able to see the parts as well as the whole, the fine details as well as the big-picture vision that makes for truly extraordinary leaders. We can even see points of commonality between things that on the surface seem opposite.

a. Oxford dictionary contributors, "equanimity," *Oxford English Dictionary,* http://www.oed.com/view/Entry/63711?redirectedFrom=equanimity#eid.

b. Jack Kornfield, "Finding the Middle Way," Jack Kornfield, https://jackkornfield.com/finding-the-middle-way/.

c. New World Encyclopedia contributors, "golden mean," *New World Encyclopedia,* http://www.newworldencyclopedia.org/entry/Golden_mean_(philosophy).

d. Kornfield, "Finding the Middle Way."

career—indeed, we've spent considerable time on it within these pages. I certainly want career satisfaction for myself, my colleagues, and the leaders I work with. But paradoxically, dissatisfaction is often what you need to find contentment.

Keep the Value of Dissatisfaction. Take a look at Mark. Some of his feelings of dissatisfaction and angst kept him motivated and on a continual quest for improvement. This makes perfect sense; if you're fully satisfied with your development and your performance, there's little incentive to grow and improve.

Dissatisfaction, rather than being a sign of failure or viewed as a shortcoming ("If I were on the right track, I wouldn't feel so dissatisfied"), should be seen as a powerful message. It can tell us we're ready for a next chapter in life, or it can be a signal to a team that the organization is ready for its next transformation. As with Quadrant II in the purpose quadrants, dissatisfaction may be the cue that it's time to expand your role or move on altogether. Or maybe it's a signal that you need to upgrade or realign to one of the Ps. Whatever it is, dissatisfaction is a signal to pay attention, and it is almost always a harbinger of progress or change. Innovation and progress are born from dissatisfaction. If you're like many leaders, including myself, you're wired to experience dissatisfaction more easily than most—and this is partly because you like to achieve, take things to the next level, and strive to push past your own perceived limits.

All of this said, when there is no contentment to temper our dissatisfaction, we become mired in constant negativity, like the leader who found herself "endlessly complaining." We see the glass as perpetually half empty, and we get stuck in that gap that led Mark to return to coaching—that space where we're neither really here nor there. It's a common experience, actually, to get stuck longing for the past or living with an eye toward some promised land where we convince ourselves that everything will be perfect. Our brains are wired to move toward pleasure and away from pain—or toward the easy route and away from that which takes effort. The goal is to keep the creative and transformative benefits of dissatisfaction while also being able to taste the contentment of what is occurring right now.

Set an Internal Barometer for "What's Enough." In a world of countless choice and everyone telling you that more is better, the next part of finding contentment is setting an *internal* barometer for what is enough. This is a completely subjective question with no single, concrete answer, but I think it's something that every leader must consider. Almost every pitfall noted in chapter 1 stems from a loss of connection to an internal barometer of what is enough, and to an inner self-confidence and humility that knows that we already are enough.

With all things—even our strengths and our greatest pleasures—there is a tipping point when the law of diminishing returns kicks in. Self-awareness helps us understand when the upsides of any given thing hit a plateau. Tap into your inner spectator to simply observe, without judgment, all the places in your work and home life where you can identify a tipping point. Here are some examples to get you started:

- Organizational or functional scorecards: What are the top three to five items that are most material?

- Last deliverable or work product: What was the right stopping point?

- Last networking event: What was enough?

- Last meal: At what point were you physically satisfied?

- Last vacation: What was the ratio of activity to rest? What was enough?

- Home: What activities reflect who you are today and are actually necessary? What is enough?

- Kids' schedules and activities: What is actually enough? What is too much?

What's enough is different at different stages of life, and even from day to day. Only you know where that line is for yourself. But the practice of asking yourself what is enough is critical, as it is far too easy to allow our comparing minds to find external barometers for that answer. One of the most heartfelt writings I have ever read on this concept comes from my dear colleague Stephen Blyth, a professor at Harvard University and former CEO of Harvard Management Company. In an article for the *Boston Globe*, Stephen explained how his journey with cancer led him to understand what is truly enough. "Months earlier I had been a chief executive overseeing 275 people and billions of dollars," Stephen wrote. "Now the prospect of the electricity bill overwhelmed me." His lowest point arrived near the end of chemotherapy treatments as he was scheduled to return to teaching. His oncologist had assured him he was physically ready, but Stephen felt so overwhelmed that "the idea of lecturing seemed utterly fanciful." A social worker at Dana-Farber helped him accept the moment for what it was—and then take appropriate action. In short, she helped him see the *one* thing that needed doing in that moment. She helped him see what was enough.[6]

Namely, all he had to do in that moment was arrange a meeting with his teaching fellows. And to make that happen, he needed to send an email. "It's all you need to do this week," the social worker pointed out. "She knew it was all that I could do," Stephen wrote. "It was enough. I sent the e-mail, and felt the first stirrings of self-compassion, a word whose meaning I was only beginning to grasp." That was the beginning of Stephen's total recovery—physically and otherwise. After his first lecture he found himself thoroughly exhausted. But again, someone arrived with just the right word: "You are teaching with chemo?" a colleague said. "That is . . . unbelievable. That is way more than enough!" That became Stephen's mantra: "teaching and chemo is More Than Enough."[7]

While you may not face a life-threatening illness like Stephen, it's safe to say that we'll all reach points where we wonder if we can go on, and wonder what's enough. We can all learn from Stephen's wisdom of being fully present to ourselves, calibrating what is enough with self-compassion, and living life as fully as we are able. When life seems to be coming at us from all sides and we feel we've reached our maximum capacity, it can be a lifesaver to remember that what's truly enough is simply the *one* thing you need to do next.

Add an Attitude of Gratitude. Just as much as it comes from knowing what's enough, contentment comes from being grateful for what we have. Even if you have big goals you still want to achieve, working toward them shouldn't come at the exclusion of being grateful for what you already have now. In fact, research has consistently shown that gratitude is good for our physical and mental well-being and also has tremendous benefits for accelerating and enhancing performance. People who feel grateful are more willing to help others, are more patient, and have greater reserves of willpower.[8] Experiments have shown that when people feel grateful, they are twice as willing to forgo an immediate smaller profit so they can invest it for a longer-term gain. Gratitude even has a beneficial social effect: people who feel and express gratitude tend to show enhanced feelings of social connection and relationship satisfaction.[9]

Researcher and bestselling author Shawn Achor has written and spoken extensively on the topic of gratitude. Achor's team found that the brain simply works better when we're feeling positive and optimistic—and that one of the best ways to feel positive and optimistic is to cultivate gratitude. A practice "as simple as writing down three things you're grateful for every day for 21 days in a row significantly increases your level of optimism, and it holds for the next six months," Achor said.[10] And increased optimism and positivity even translate into better performance and better bottom-line results. Achor summarizes some of the research: workers who scored low on a life satisfaction test stay home an average of 1.25 more days per month, which translates to a decrease in productivity of fifteen days per year. Moreover, Gallup researchers found that retail stores whose employees had higher life satisfaction scores generated $21 more in earnings per square foot of space than other stores, adding $32 million in additional profits for the whole chain.[11]

One of the most powerful descriptions of gratitude I've ever read comes from Alan Morinis, author of *Everyday Holiness*. A participant in a leadership development program introduced me to this book, and it's one that I've really come to treasure. Says Morinis on gratitude and its power:

ADD AN ATTITUDE OF GRATITUDE NOW

- Stop reading and write down three things you are grateful for at this exact moment.

- Notice what you experience as the shift to a Leader A lens brings focus to what you are grateful for.

- If this practice is fruitful for you, keep it up. Jot down three "gratitudes" a day, and periodically pause to check in and reflect on how the practice is supporting you.

Practicing gratitude means being fully aware of the good that is already yours. . . . Gratitude can't co-exist with arrogance, resentment, and selfishness. . . . Yet gratitude doesn't come easily to us, and it usually takes some effort to develop this quality through practice. When we practice gratitude, we make an effort to heighten our awareness of the gifts we already possess and so relieve ourselves of the exhausting pursuit of the ever-receding targets of those things we think we lack. No wonder gratitude satisfies the soul. It frees us from compulsive grasping, and so gives us back our lives.[12]

As I have considered how to cultivate more contentment in my own life, I've created a mantra to use whenever I start to feel over-whelmed, stressed, or tempted to take on more than I should. In those cases, I try to bring some self-compassion and say to myself: "Let me have the humility to know what's enough, the gratitude to see that it's all enough, and the peace within to know that I am enough."

#3: *Trust* in Self and Life in the Moment

The third part of ACT is meeting the moment with a greater trust in yourself and in life. The reality is you've been successful in the past, you've met incredible leadership goals and challenges in the past, and as long as you understand your own success cycle, you'll do it again. In the midst of being in Leader B mode, it's easy to lose sight of the wins of the past as well as the fundamental capacity you have and will always have to learn, grow, and adapt. Trust in self and life is part of tapping into Leader A, who can see this bigger picture.

Get Updated to Who You Are as a Leader Now. Let's look back to Mark. While part of his DNA was to be a bit anxious about performance and improvement—and he could leverage that unease to fuel and support core values such as humility, hard work, and the grit to keep going—he had gone over the tipping point. What was previously helpful was now hindering him from being the leader he wanted to be. Mark needed to update his understanding of who he was and where he was as a leader *now*. It almost felt like there were times when Mark still saw himself as that younger banker he was from years ago instead of fully embracing and owning the seasoned executive he now was.

I was recently with a group of fifty executives at a retreat. Their boss opened the retreat by asking the group to share what they would change from the previous year, without remorse or regret. To my surprise, over half the executives said they wished they had trusted their gut and intuition (or as this group called it, their "belly barometers") more. Many described knowing it was time to let someone go, or knowing it was time to make a certain investment, and rather than pulling the trigger, they dragged their feet on it.

One CEO I worked with pointed out the importance for leaders to embrace what he called "the paradox of paranoia and trust." He described how he and his executive team always held "a healthy level of paranoia" that kept them on their toes *as well as* a deep level of trust that they had hit major milestones before, and they would do so again.

As with all things, balance is necessary. What this CEO meant by "healthy paranoia" could be described as vigilance, focus, and attention to detail. But in excess, it's hypervigilance, obsession, tunnel vision, or getting lost in the details. At this end of the spectrum, unhealthy paranoia shifts us to a Leader B lens and a "mindset of scarcity" where we don't trust that the next sale will come in or that we'll reach the next goal. We don't trust our colleagues, and we don't trust that others will think we're adding value or know that we are capable. We telegraph to the world that we're in it for ourselves at all costs and become preoccupied with trying to prove that we're the smartest in the room. Or, we telegraph our insecurity and become preoccupied with grasping for some kind of acknowledgment or nod that we're okay.

And while perhaps the majority of driven, ambitious leaders don't find themselves going to the other extreme with trust, it's certainly possible. Trust taken to the extreme—or assuming that things will somehow "magically" work out—can lead to complacency, stagnation, and underperformance. This end of the spectrum may not be as common, but it's a great reminder than *anything* in excess can go awry.

The bottom line here? Building more trust to balance our self-doubt and our self-preservation requires that we take some time to stay updated on who and where we are now as leaders. We can look back to our results and our experience and know that we did well—and trust that we will do so again.

Engage in a Chapters Review. One exercise I've developed to help leaders look back and gain a wide-angle, Leader A perspective on their leadership journey is a tool called the Chapters Review, which is where I began with Mark. Like a business that does a quarterly review, we sit down together in a safe and private space and look back on all the chapters of the leader's life and career.

We rarely take the time to really examine each chapter of our lives, and we miss out on fully integrating the role that each chapter has played in shaping who we are, what we know, what values are important to us, and who we are as people, professionals, and leaders. Given the lightning speed at which most organizations operate, it's not surprising that we seldom pause for such a comprehensive retrospective. But slowing down and making time to look at what has transpired to date is invaluable. If spectating yourself is cultivating self-awareness in the moment, the Chapters Review is a concentrated exercise in big-picture self-awareness. It gives you the opportunity to look at all the pieces together and see how each has informed and amplified the rest.

Harvard Business School professor Lakshmi Ramarajan says that the process of learning, growing, and developing an integrated self is one of construction and meaning-making. As leaders explore their life stories and process their experiences, they develop a deeper understanding of themselves—of who they are and how they came to be that person. Ramarajan says that this is a lifelong journey in which we are always discovering the next layer, "much like peeling an onion."[13]

Chapters Review Exercise

Following is a table that can help you engage in a Chapters Review exercise. You don't have to use the chapters as defined here; if something doesn't resonate, feel free to strike it, or if something is missing, feel free to add it. Part of the value of this exercise is actually seeing how you define your unique chapters.

If you are able to share your results with another person, consider working with a coach, trusted advisor, or personal confidante. Have them listen for themes and patterns. Often, an objective observer can identify insights we wouldn't necessarily see. I've used this exercise

TABLE 6-1

The Chapters Review table

Define your own chapters here (use the following as illustrations)	High school (or previous)	College	Early career	Midcareer	Current day
Impact and contributions (e.g., at work, at home, or in the broader community)					
Memorable or meaningful events, achievements, or people during this time					
Strengths utilized or skills gained					
Life or leadership lessons that shaped who you are, defined your values clearly, or helped to build your resilience					
How you made meaning of your life in each stage or chapter (the lens you held)					
High points and low points					
What gave you energy, "juice," or inspiration					
What drained you, and what left you feeling inauthentic or exhausted					
Any Achilles' heels during this time (and in which P)					
How you knew it was time for a new chapter— what demarked a chapter shift					

with leaders at every stage of career and from widely diverse industries, and invariably, it's yielded powerful "aha moments."

Remember Who You Are. For some professionals, the Chapters Review reminds them of who they are at their core—beyond what they're producing. We can become so focused on results that it's easy to forget who we are at the level of being versus the level of doing—and that we are complex individuals who are so much more than our current job.

One leader named one of his chapters the Soccer Chapter and shared how important soccer had been in his life from childhood through college, and how those early experiences defined so much of who he was now and how he viewed things. He realized that with less time now, he had lost touch with the athlete part of himself, and it was a part that he wanted to tap back into. We discussed how to add that back in—from joining an adult soccer league to attending local matches or even getting together with friends to watch soccer on TV. Anything that would take him back into that realm that had been so life-giving and energizing was a positive step.

For Mark, the Chapters Review exercise was liberating. The best thing to emerge from it was realizing he truly wasn't interested in being anyone other than himself. He gained a great deal of energy from describing each of his chapters and recounting the skills and knowledge he'd gained from each new role, the results he'd delivered, and the contributions he'd made to others' careers. He realized that the common denominator throughout every chapter in his life, from as far back as middle school, was his natural curiosity and capacity to learn. He had, as he put it, "a healthy compulsion" to figure things out.

In fact, the Chapters Review highlighted for Mark that he was someone who thrived on new learning curves—he really needed them to feel meaning and fulfillment in life. So rather than come at the next challenge with the same level of stress or worry, he had greater confidence that as he had before, he'd figure out this next role and challenge just the same. He said that after doing the Chapters Review, he could ease up on the need to prove himself. It showed him he actually had a great track record, and he had every reason to believe that he'd continue on his current trajectory of success. Free of that worry, now he could concentrate on areas where he felt he could make a deeper, more lasting impact, such as mentoring others in his organization, or spending more time with his family.

See the "So What." The Chapters Review also widens our Leader A lens by helping us see how former jobs, negative experiences, or even great disappointments that may not have made sense to us at the time actually have a greater purpose. A recent client who just completed his Chapters Review shared his excitement about an upcoming business opportunity. He said he could now see how everything that had previously transpired in his career and life seemed to be preparing him for this exact moment in time. This is the kind of realization that simply isn't possible without taking the time to pause and reflect on the totality of our experience.

A leader who started her own successful business recounted how one of the lowest points in her life was actually the springboard for her current successful, happy career. Previously, she'd worked for a terrible boss and in a toxic work environment. Before the Chapters Review, she'd looked on that chapter of her life with regret—as wasted years. But now she had a new lens and could see how those experiences planted the seed for the work she does today. "It took *that* level of pain in a job to spark the courage I needed to become an entrepreneur and start my own business," she said.

A deeper knowing and peace arise as you realize that every job, every experience that preceded where you are today, whether good or bad, has value. What you once viewed as a negative experience can, through a fresh lens, reveal itself as the stepping-stone that got you where you are today. When someone says to make the most of life or the moment, I've increasingly come to think that this means embracing and accepting the full lot of it. When we numb out and avoid one side of the equation, invariably we lose out on the other. When we avoid our pain, we dull our joy as well.

The Chapters Review brings leaders fully up to speed on who and where they are. As leaders recount the chapters, most often they are floored by how much they have grown and expanded. They see how often they have redefined and realigned their Ps at many different stages of life. And the exercise infuses some additional trust and faith in yourself: you always have the capacity to keep growing and learning and aligning and realigning to your Ps as often as necessary.

Transition from Striving to Greater Meaning and Purpose

As I've seen others work through the parts of ACT, it's incredible when I start to sense that their tight grip on things begins to loosen. They move from self-protective, defensive plays to more offensive plays, where they can be both focused and relaxed. They come to better understand that leadership development is about becoming the next best versions of themselves.

Give Yourself Permission to Thrive. Once our grip has loosened, I think it's easier to give ourselves permission to enjoy the ride and to make decisions for our lives based on who and what gives us meaning, what feeds us, and what is true to the larger path and purpose we are called to. It's okay now to rest, to play, to love, to feel joy, and to make choices based on what gives us meaning and a deep sense of fulfillment. The loud "should" voice that has pushed us along at earlier points has done its work and can now fall silent. As Mary Oliver said in her incredible poem "Wild Geese":

> *You do not have to walk on your knees*
> *For a hundred miles through the desert, repenting.*
> *You only have to let the soft animal of your body*
> *love what it loves.*[14]

Have Principles Drive Leadership Action. As Mark worked his way through ACT, he was excited to consider how his leadership actions going forward could now more consistently stem from a set of core principles instead of the historic need to prove or outdo himself. Less pulled by the whiplash of extremes, Mark wanted to be a true steward of the resources he had and the role he was in.

While his leadership actions might not have looked different to outsiders, Mark now found himself regularly pausing to consider the purpose driving his behaviors and to what end he was engaging in an action. As Eiji Toyoda, the Toyota Motor Corporation's former president, once said about wise leadership: "To do what you

TABLE 6-2

What are your foundations of leadership?

Lead from a place of self-preservation (Leader B)	Leadership action	Lead from a core set of principles (Leader A)
• Prove you're the smartest in the room	Demonstrate knowledge	• Share judgment to get to best answer • Mentor others
• Protect identity of "good person" • Avoid conflict • People please	Give	• Pay it forward • Do the right thing • Be a servant leader
• Protect territory or status • Desire to one-up self or other	Build	• Lead progress and innovation • Create more opportunity for all
• Avoid boredom or painful feelings • Indulge in the shiny and new	Seek variety	• Learn • Grow
• Avoid risk for fear of making a mistake • Control or be overly critical • Create unnecessary bureaucracy	Bring order/discipline	• Be a steward of resources • Ensure justice and fairness

believe is right. To do what you believe is good. Doing the right things, when required, is a calling from on high. Do it boldly, do as you believe, do as you are."[15]

Table 6-2 shows the distinctions between leading from a place of striving and leading from a place of core principles. There is a thin line between the two, and of course we won't always have the perfect batting average. But being aware of what differentiates the two helps us know when we are operating from our highest and best Leader A mode and when we are not.

Accept the Ultimate Paradox: Honor Self to Transcend Self. As we come to the close of this chapter, let's look at the ultimate paradox I've observed in working with leaders. As they work with the five Ps, what begins as an exercise in self-awareness and self-care in order to understand the conditions that help them be more effective, present, and satisfied leads them to a place where they feel ready to be in service of something bigger than themselves. Here is what happens each time we align to a P:

- With purpose, we reset the compass and point to where our passions and contributions lie now, cultivating a greater courage and conviction to prioritize the highest and best use of our time and energy.

- With process, we honor our natural rhythms and routines, setting up structures and rituals that align to what matters most to us, and protect our time and energy for those things.

- With people, we surround ourselves with good people, raising our game while raising the game of others, and ensuring that we and others have the support we need to keep growing and flourishing.

- With presence, we stay focused and embrace the full range of emotions within us without running away or indulging in excess, and instead are more present to the full range of our experiences.

- With peace, we come to see that we have developed the capacities to evolve, adapt, and respond to whatever comes our way, and we see and accept that we have enough and are enough, deepening inner confidence and strength.

Cultivating and understanding who we are as Leader A and the underlying conditions that support our highest and best creates the foundation to transcend the self and be in service of a purpose or mission greater than ourselves. It's this kind of foundation that enables servant leadership and leaders who are truly paying it forward. By regularly choosing to cultivate our best selves, we grow into the leaders we want to be.

At some point, like Mark, we find that we no longer need to lead from a place of deficit or striving; rather, we hear more clearly the beat of a drum that comes from a wider perspective and the understanding that our unique, authentic path is a gift we've been given.

When you've attained a certain level of external and internal power and success, the question then becomes, how will you use what you have responsibly and in service of something beyond yourself?

Leadership development and growth will always include some dimension of adding more technical skill, increasing one's knowledge of the business or industry, and improving the softer skills, such as interpersonal or communications skills. However, as one becomes more seasoned and competent, and as one achieves more success, space opens for broader questions to come into play. Research has shown that leadership development tends to move from self-focused questions such as, "What's in it for me, and how can I achieve my goals?" to "How can I create a shared vision that will transform myself and my organization?" all the way to, at the highest (and rarest) levels of leadership development, "How can I effect society-wide transformation?"[16] Leaders move beyond an individualistic stance that concentrates on power and self-benefit to a far more expansive view that considers existential questions regarding life vocation, purpose, meaning, and giving back.

At the most advanced stages of leadership development, we find visionary leaders who are calm, focused, and peaceful within and without, even in the face of immense responsibility and enormous demands on their time and energy. These are the leaders who, according to researchers and authors David Rooke and William Torbert, possess "an extraordinary capacity to deal simultaneously with many situations at multiple levels," and "can deal with immediate priorities yet never lose sight of long-term goals." On a daily basis, though these leaders are engaged in multiple initiatives or even multiple organizations, they aren't "in a constant rush—nor [do] they devote hours on end to a single activity."[17] These leaders—whom Rooke and Torbert call Alchemists—are living examples of *wu-wei*, the concept of "effortless action" we learned back in the introduction.

Fascinatingly, leaders at this stage of development exhibit paradoxes at every turn. They are extraordinarily productive yet rarely appear busy or rushed. They can inspire change on an organizational or even societal level yet still connect with and inspire individual employees. They are equally at home in a grand vision and the granular level needed to make that vision a reality, yet they never get lost in the clouds or bogged down in the details. And they tend to be, despite their incredible achievements, humble.

Pioneering leadership expert Jim Collins calls the kind of leader we've been discussing a Level 5 executive, and one of their chief characteristics is this "powerful mixture of personal humility plus professional will." Level 5 executives (like Rooke and Torbert's Alchemists) possess enormous ambition—but, as Collins points out, first and foremost, it's ambition on behalf of their organizations and causes, not themselves. They are leaders so successful they have scaled the ranks of their companies or industries or even society at large, but they prefer to lead from a relative place of obscurity. They aren't in the game for money, power, fame, or anything else that is merely self-serving. They are motivated by big-picture impact; they have become successful individually, to be sure, but for the good of the whole.[18]

Research further shows that the rising leaders of the millennial generation—an educated and culturally diverse group expected to compose 50 percent of the workforce by 2020—are asking the big questions at an earlier stage of career than their predecessors. Trends show that "[m]illennial workers are more likely to look for meaning and impact in their work and aren't satisfied simply punching a clock," and that they place a higher value on helping someone in need than on a high-paying career.[19] In some ways, then, they're beginning their careers with the bigger questions of service, meaning, and purpose—and good thing, as employees who feel inspired and deeply engaged in their company's mission are more than twice as productive as their counterparts, and derive far more meaning and satisfaction from their jobs.[20]

No matter your age or generational cohort, at some point in your career, these deeper, big-picture questions will eventually come up, and they are crucial to contemplate as you think about your well-being, sustainability, and long-term development as a leader.

What makes work meaningful? The answers are unique to each of us, but the results of one recent study found five characteristics that are common to meaningful work:

1. IT'S SELF-TRANSCENDENT. It benefits and is relevant to people other than oneself.

2. IT'S POIGNANT. It taps into our emotions, and not just positive ones. Researchers found that it was dealing with the challenging moments that tended to make work more meaningful.

3. IT'S EPISODIC. A sense of meaning arises from peak experiences. While the peak experience doesn't last, the memory of it does and is incorporated into a person's life narrative.

4. IT'S REFLECTIVE. Meaningfulness is rarely experienced in the midst of a peak experience but rather later, upon reflection (such as in a Chapters Review).

5. IT'S PERSONAL. While things like impact and effectiveness tend to be relegated to work, a sense of meaningful work goes beyond the office doors and connects with one's personal life (for example, when a family member is proud of what you do or you become aware of how your work helps people in the community).[21]

How do we create the conditions that make meaningful work possible? We come full circle to our first P, purpose. We come back to the deeper, more aspirational aspects of work that tap into our highest and best use, and to our passion that contributes to meaning and to our long-term sustainability as a leader.

What to Remember:

➤ As we reach a certain level of success, the fifth P, peace, helps us to relax and give ourselves permission to feel a greater satisfaction in the leadership experience. Rather than holding on so tightly and being defensive, we shift to the offense, loosening our grip just enough that we can enjoy the ride along the way.

➤ Peace doesn't need to be an abstract or soft concept. You can use the acronym of ACT as a reminder to incorporate peace into your leadership experience. The A is about *accepting* the

moment so you can save time and energy by taking constructive and effective action for what's within your control with
more ease and acceleration. The C is about being *content* in
the moment, knowing what's enough and bringing more of
an attitude of gratitude. The T is increasing your *trust* in
yourself and life, knowing that you've achieved, learned, and
grown, and you will again.

➤ As you increase your acceptance, contentment, and trust,
your leadership actions stem less from a need to prove
yourself, self-preserve, or one-up others or yourself in some
way. Leadership actions are then able to flow more consistently from a set of core principles that benefit not only the
leader but their teams and organizations as well.

➤ Leaders at peace have the humility to know what's enough,
the gratitude to see that it's all enough, and the peace within
to know that they are enough.

➤ As leaders develop a strong and healthy internal sense of self,
they find that all the focus on honoring oneself shifts to the
ability to transcend oneself. At later stages of leadership
development, the highest-functioning leaders begin to ask not
just "What's in it for me?" but also questions such as, "How
can I transform my team, my organization, or even society at
large?" Paying it forward and servant leadership move to the
forefront at this stage of development.

CHAPTER SEVEN

Pay It Forward

Create Leader A Teams and Organizations

We ended the last chapter on peace describing how as leaders widen their lens, ease up on the "shoulds," and act less from a place of striving, they're able to act more regularly from a place of meaning and purpose. The most high-functioning, effective, present, and satisfied leaders have moved beyond asking, "What's in it for me?" or even "How can I do that stronger or better?" to questions such as, "How can I be of service to others and help transform my team, my organization, or society at large?"

It takes a certain level of inner confidence and a healthy sense of one's highest and best self to be able to arrive at a place where concepts such as servant leadership and paying it forward move to the forefront. While many authors have written about the concept of servant leadership, one of the best definitions still comes from Robert Greenleaf, who coined the phrase in an essay published back in 1970. In it, Greenleaf writes, "The servant-leader is servant first. . . . It begins with that natural feeling that one wants to serve. The best test, which is difficult to administer, is: Do those served grow as persons? Do they, while being served, become healthier, wiser, freer, more autonomous, more likely themselves to become servants?"[1]

Here in our final chapter, we will delve into the positive impact you can have on your teams and organizations by choosing Leader A for yourself and helping others to do the same. I will first share why it's critical to recognize your own ripple effect and how choosing Leader A goes well beyond your own satisfaction and effectiveness. Then, we'll look at the state of organizations today and what you can do to develop more Leader A leaders, teams, and organizations. I'll end the chapter—and the book—with a final vision and call to action that I hope will help you nurture Leader A in yourself for the long term and inspire others to do the same.

Don't Underestimate Your Ripple Effect: Choose a Positive Legacy

One of the biggest responsibilities of leadership is the effect we have on others. As a leader, you are the standard bearer, the one out front, the example everyone sees and emulates. You are the one who sets goals, objectives, and deadlines, and you are also the one who sets the tone, the culture, and the general ethos of your work environment. And the more senior, the more high performing, and the more visible you are as a leader, the greater the effect you have.[2]

If you call to mind the visual of a pebble dropped into a lake, you've got an apt image of how leadership begins from that one point—you—and flows out in ever-widening circles to touch team members, divisions, organizations, shareholders, and, depending on how high your profile is, entire industries or communities. What do you want that ripple effect to look like and feel like for others? Depending on which mode you're in, Leader A or Leader B, you'll have a very different impact. Beyond the negative consequences of Leader B mode on your own stress levels, effectiveness, and health, your Leader B mode also negatively impacts whole teams of people (direct reports or colleagues or both), or even whole organizations.

Like a set of dominoes, your Leader B "ripple" cascades out to affect anyone you work with, creating more Leader B days for others.

As I shared in chapter 1 on the pitfalls to performance, when you,
the leader, are focused on just doing more (*with no prioritization
and focus on the value you add*), on doing it now and telegraphing
a state of emergency (*without an appropriate discernment or clarity on the true level of urgency*), on doing it yourself (*creating bottlenecks, being in the weeds, and micromanaging*), or on just doing
it later (*putting off caring of your health and well-being*), it's not
only you who suffers but also your loved ones, your teams, your
organizations, and ultimately the mission and goals you hope to
achieve.

Without self-awareness, it's all too easy to affect others with a
negative attitude or unintentionally foster an atmosphere that undermines our team's effectiveness. Remember that our unresolved
inner conflicts (such as the need to prove ourselves, people-please,
one-up others, or control others) inevitably play out in our outer
world too—at work and at home. Armed with self-knowledge,
however, we can take whatever steps we need to in order to become the very best leader we were meant to be, in any context.

Fortunately, the ripple effect holds true for Leader A as well. The
more continuously you feed Leader A, the greater your positive effect.
According to a recent Gallup research report that surveyed 105 teams
over six three-month periods, researchers found that the well-being
of team members is directly dependent on the well-being of others on
the team—and that the effect increases over time. Individual team
members who reported experiencing what researchers called "thriving well-being" in the first round of the study were 20 percent more
likely to have thriving team members six months later.[3]

The ripple effect isn't confined to the workplace, of course—
leaders take their jobs home with them, and it's worth remembering your team members do as well. This puts even more responsibility
on leaders to be mindful of their ripple effect and to take measures
to continuously feed and support Leader A. Professor Clayton
Christensen beautifully captured this dynamic in his classic article,
"How Will You Measure Your Life?":

> *In my mind's eye I saw one of my managers leave for work one morning with a relatively strong level of self-esteem. Then, I pictured her driving home to her family 10 hours later, feeling unappreciated, frustrated, underutilized, and demeaned. I imagined how profoundly her lowered self-esteem affected the way she interacted with her children. The vision in my mind then fast-forwarded to another day, when she drove home with greater self-esteem—feeling that she had learned a lot, had been recognized for achieving valuable things, and had played a significant role in the success of some important initiatives. I then imagined how positively that affected her as a spouse and a parent. My conclusion: Management is the most noble of professions if it's practiced well. No other occupation offers as many ways to help others learn and grow, take responsibility, be recognized for achievement, and contribute to the success of a team.*[4]

Practiced well, leadership is an art form that carries with it the potential to profoundly affect others—it is indeed a high calling. One senior leader I know who works in a federal agency chooses to look at her ripple effect and her overall purpose and effectiveness through the lens of her legacy. She shared that as she thought about the legacy she hopes to create for her organization and for her family, she has made a practice of asking herself each day upon awaking, "Am I choosing to be a blessing for others today?" This practice has helped set each day in the right direction, and it helps her make individual decisions. This is the way she feeds Leader A.

Consider for a moment how you can make that question work for you. "Am I choosing to be . . . a role model for others today? An inspiration for others? An agent of change who has improved the lives of others? A calm presence in the midst of the fray? A visionary who keeps the whole team on course?" There are as many answers as there are leaders—and over the course of our careers, we will be called on to wear many hats. Part of the responsibility of leadership practiced well is having the self-awareness to know the best way to pay it forward for any given situation and in any context.

Develop Leader A Leaders, Teams, and Organizations

As you think about the positive legacy you hope to create as a leader of your organization, team, and home, I hope that you will be a leader who proactively and consciously thinks about setting up conditions that help others to discover and cultivate the Leader A within themselves. This is part of our calling as leaders.

But let's keep it real here: many leaders find themselves in contexts that, frankly, skew toward feeding Leader B. I frequently hear from leaders who describe processes that keep them in Leader B mode, or who are working within a Leader B company culture. With all the challenges, complexities, and problems facing organizations and the world today, what we need now are leaders who are willing to stand up and change the zeitgeist. Who are willing to work to reverse the trend toward stress and overwork, and all the other conditions that keep workers locked in Leader B mode, with all its subsequent pitfalls.

Here are four actionable things you can start with today.

#1: Create a Shared Language Using "Leader A" and "Leader B" with Your Teams

I developed the heuristic of "Leader A" and "Leader B" as a way to help leaders process, make sense of, and describe the complexity of what they were experiencing. Within the coaching setting, the nomenclature provided my clients and me with a way to talk about, track, and better understand:

- The conditions that feed and align to their highest and best when they feel especially effective, present, and satisfied (Leader A mode)

- The conditions that lead to feeling their worst—stressed, overwhelmed, or negative, where their effectiveness, presence, and satisfaction are limited or compromised (Leader B mode, and the pitfalls that come with it)

In the same way that there is value for a coach and a leader to have this shared language, so too is there value for you to have this shared language between you and your direct reports or team members. (It's also been a great tool for HR or talent leaders.)

One client, for example, used the language of Leader A and Leader B in a team retreat for his direct reports. He had called the meeting because he sensed falling morale, burnout, and high stress throughout the division. After a brief explanation of the Leader A and Leader B framework, the group had a concrete and objective way to organize their discussion.

They were able to acknowledge the parts of the business and their jobs that would naturally make for Leader B days. One by one, they had the opportunity to honestly share their ratios of Leader A to Leader B days and the conditions that led to each. The group then worked together to brainstorm ways to shift the A:B ratio, not only for their division but especially for those colleagues who were experiencing the worst ratios at the time. The group devised ways to create fewer Leader B days for their teams and to watch out for their own behaviors that could be driving Leader B days for others. With their conversation framed around the concept of Leader A and Leader B, they were able to have an honest dialogue about what they were each experiencing, what they needed from each other, and what support they needed from their boss.

By the end of their day together, this group felt closer and more cohesive. One participant put it like this: "I feel like our team is more of a 'we' now rather than a 'we versus me.' The Leader A and Leader B framework showed us we have so many common experiences." This group of peers typically spent their retreats focusing on business issues or doing team building by taking personality assessments or talking about style differences. This time, they felt they were getting real with each other about the stresses, complexities, and challenges they were facing.

I've seen these same outcomes even for leaders who don't work together every day. I've facilitated retreats for executives from across many different companies and industries, and I have seen the productive dialogue that can come from something as simple as asking people about their ratio of Leader A to Leader B days, or to describe who they are when they are operating on all cylinders as their highest and best Leader A. The buzz and energy in the room suggests there is a common set of experiences we are all having as leaders in trying to do our best in a climate marked by speed, change, and complexity—experiences that need to be addressed head-on.

#2: Don't Normalize Leader B; Get to the Root Cause

By having language for and a definition of what Leader A and Leader B look like for your team, you have a neutral language with which to discuss some tough issues. Part of our responsibility as leaders is to disallow any toxic Leader B behavior in the organization. Toxic behavior undermines morale, productivity, team cohesion, and the positive development of all team members. And because of the ripple effect, it *will* spread from one to many. If you see a colleague or team member in a string of Leader B days or in a full-blown pitfall, you have a responsibility to give that person feedback and to help coach them through it. The Leader A and B framework makes giving feedback easier, more objective, and less personalized, and it gives you an effective way to avoid normalizing Leader B.

Remember that we all get off track from time to time, so bring some compassion and put on your "manager-as-coach" hat to support someone in getting back to Leader A mode more quickly and with less damage. Even those with the most egregious, uncivil behavior need the support of their managers, and quite often, when you get to the root cause of their behaviors, what you find is they are overloaded, inordinately stressed, or insecure.

Research from Christine Porath, associate professor of management at Georgetown University, supports this observation. Porath has spent much of her career examining incivility in the workplace. In her book *Mastering Civility*, Porath says that uncivil behaviors such as emailing during meetings or interrupting others, all the way to more extreme behaviors such as belittling others, are on the rise. In her research, fully 95 percent of survey respondents believed that civility is a problem in the United States, and 70 percent said incivility had reached crisis proportions. The most common reason people gave for poor behavior, Porath asserts, was the feeling of being over-loaded or stressed.[5]

Obviously, boorish, arrogant, or any other uncivil behavior in the workplace creates a toxic work environment and can't con-tinue. But remembering that the root cause is likely to be stress and overwork gives you a way to effectively address the situation and facilitate real change. If one of your direct reports seems es-pecially overwhelmed, stressed, or unable to scale into a larger role, or is demonstrating negative behavior, meet one on one and clearly and objectively share your observations. You can use the language of the pitfalls to help shift his or her lens from Leader B to Leader A:

- I see that you're handling a lot of volume (Just Do More Pitfall) → let's make sure what you're doing is your highest and best value-add.

- There are a lot of fire drills happening lately (Just Do It Now Pitfall) → let's look at your team's scorecard and discuss what's truly a priority.

- You're taking on a lot of the load from your team (Just Do It Myself Pitfall) → let's talk about how to reset your level of involvement and make sure you're getting the leverage you need and that the team is empowered to do their job.

- I'm worried that you're just doing what's most urgent instead of what's most important (Just Do It Later Pitfall) → let's look at what we can put on the back burner or deprioritize to get your focus back on the most important things.

Then, use the five Ps to help the person create a plan of action, as shown in table 7-1.

If the low performance or negative behavior persists, then you may need to go back to chapter 4 on people to remember that

TABLE 7-1

The five P path to a Leader A mindset

Which P?	Possible actions to take
Purpose	• Get clear on the most critical tangible and intangible contributions
	• Use the passion-contribution quadrants to help reset priorities
	• Review strategic yesses, partial yesses, and nos
Process	• Realign tasks to energy for burst-tasking vs. steady as she goes
	• Reinforce power hours, calendar coding, and better use of white space
	• Encourage restoration rituals
People	• Look at current team structure and capabilities
	• Assess the current leverage-empower-inspire ratio on the team
	• Encourage reaching out to others for support
Presence	• Name the Achilles' heels
	• Identify triggers
	• Create new if-then choices and greater "choice of voice" for more situational awareness and effectiveness
Peace	• Bring perspective and widen the leader's lens to see what's in their control and what's not
	• Help to set a barometer for what's enough
	• Provide positive feedback and reassurance where possible

sometimes the most compassionate thing you can do is to take the "pitcher out of the game" and not let one person bring down the performance, morale, or effectiveness of an entire team.

#3: Be a Good Steward of Organizational Time, Energy, and Resources

Ultimately, part of leading from a place of meaning and purpose is to recognize that as a leader of a team, organization, or home, you are a steward of the time, energy, and resources of that context. One of the biggest issues in organizational life today is the feeling that there are never enough hours in the day, that there are never enough resources, and that motivation is waning. Fortunately, there are things you can do to help set up processes, norms, or structures to productively channel time, resources, and motivation. Here are some action steps to take to create conditions for others to have more Leader A days.

Be Ruthless about Prioritization: Keep the Team Focused on the Highest and Most Important Priorities. Work and priorities trickle down from above, so do all you can to help your colleagues or direct reports stay focused on what matters most and on the most important goals for the year. One CEO I worked with was brought in to help turn around an organization that had been lagging in performance. As he assessed the situation, it was clear the entire organization was mired in a lot of busy volume and activity, but there was no real prioritization from the top. He created an image of a magnifying glass that depicted their highest-priority goals, posted it everywhere in the organization to help keep everyone focused, and asked all functional heads to do the same for their areas.

When I spoke to people in the company, they said the most amazing thing about this leader was that when you had an idea, he would listen and hear you out, and his decision to move forward with the idea or not was always tied back to the magnifying glass and priorities. This was a leader who was not only committed to changing performance but also determined to get people focused to avoid becoming overworked or burnt out. A year later, the organization's performance is on an upward trend, the workforce is more motivated, and the people are working fewer hours.

Be intentional in identifying a focused, essential set of goals rather than overloading the deck, which diffuses time and energy. Hans Schulz, former CEO of Liechtenstein-based industrial company Balzers, shared in a 2010 *Harvard Business Review* article that managers "are no longer allowed to set 10 top-priority goals." While head of Balzers, he permitted managers to name just three "must-win battles," because, he pointed out, the point of goal setting isn't to pile up projects but "to give people an orientation and to focus their action, attention, and energy." After this rule went into effect, significantly more goals were achieved. To help make goal reduction stick, Schulz said, a visible commitment from the CEO is necessary—especially in companies accustomed to following a management-by-objectives approach. Leaders must help managers understand the purpose and value of refocusing on just a few goals and assist them in applying the new rules.[6]

As a leader, not only should you be asking, "Am I using my time and energy toward my highest and best use in the role?" but also asking your team that same question, over and over again.

Have Clear Decision-Making Frameworks for Go-No-Go. A few of my favorite ideas on keeping teams focused on their highest and best comes from the *Harvard Business Review* article "Help Your Team Stop Overcommitting by Empowering Them to Say No." There, Diana Kander points out that you only have enough bandwidth for the truly groundbreaking ideas and tasks if you say no to the ones that just aren't good enough. Saying no was a point of pride for Steve Jobs, for example. "As he put it at a conference in 1997," Kander writes, "'People think focus means saying yes to the thing you've got to focus on. But that's not what it means at all. It means saying no to the hundred other good ideas that there are. You have to pick carefully. I'm actually as proud of the things we haven't done as the things I have done. Innovation is saying no to 1,000 things.'"[7]

Saying no includes being able to recognize and act on what Kander calls "pivot indicators" for key initiatives and ideas. Pivot indicators are warning signs that you need to change course or pull the plug on an initiative or idea that isn't adding value. She points out that most organizations measure only success metrics, or the numbers that tell them they're doing well—how much money was raised, how close they stayed to the budget and timeline, and so on. Pivot indicators, on the other hand, answer two questions: When will we know if this doesn't work, and how will we know? Heeding pivot indicators can tell you when an adjustment needs to be made and save you untold time and resources.[8]

Leadership professors Heike Bruch and Jochen I. Menges also suggest that leaders institute "spring cleaning." While this doesn't necessarily need to happen every spring, it's smart to periodically cull lower-performing initiatives that don't contribute to the organizational goals. Some companies establish a schedule for spring cleaning; others simply decide that they'll "clean house" whenever tasks and activities seem overwhelming or before launching a new change process. At one company Bruch and Menges studied, employees were asked not for ideas for new initiatives but ideas about what could be terminated. With little effort they came up with 540 ideas! That was three times the annual number of new-project ideas they'd been suggesting, and the company ended up halting 40 percent of its projects. Bruch and Menges's advice? "Regularly ask yourself, your managers, and the whole company: 'Which of our current activities would we start now if they weren't already under way?' Then eliminate all the others."[9]

Create Cultural Norms, Processes, and Programs That Protect Productivity, Attention, and Performance. So much of the overload and stress that people feel comes from the 24-7 nature of work. Many of us are now expected to be *on* the clock *around* the clock, and in many cases, overwork is explicitly encouraged. Thankfully, many forward-looking organizations are taking steps to change the culture of overwork.

As a leader, part of our responsibility is to create cultural norms and processes that protect employees' productivity, attention, performance, and overall well-being. Vynamic, a Philadelphia healthcare consultancy, created a policy called "zmail," where email is discouraged between 10 p.m. and 7 a.m. on weekdays, and all day on weekends. The policy doesn't explicitly forbid work or communication during these times, but it does compel staff to assess whether an after-hours message is important enough to warrant a phone call. If employees do choose to work during off-hours, zmail saves the messages as drafts to be manually sent later, or they program their email client to automatically send the messages during work hours. This policy underscores Vynamic's stated belief that downtime is important and encourages employee behaviors that contribute to the culture.[10]

One organization I worked with instituted no meetings on Thursdays and encouraged folks to schedule fifty-minute meetings to give people ten-minute breaks between meetings. These short windows, during which employees could get a bite to eat or grab a cup of coffee, make a quick call, or simply enjoy a bit of downtime, did wonders for morale. It was just enough of a "recharge and reset" to clear the decks and get them ready for the next meeting's agenda.

Other companies are taking advantage of mindfulness programs to help their teams manage stress and prevent burnout. At Aetna, for example, CEO Mark Bertolini has instituted yoga and meditation classes for employees. More than one-quarter of the company's 50,000 employees have participated, and on average, they report a 28 percent reduction in their stress levels, a 20 percent improvement in sleep quality, and a 19 percent reduction in pain. They've also gained an average of 62 minutes per week of productivity, which Aetna estimates is worth $3,000 per employee per year.[11]

Take Victory Laps Together as a Team. I've heard all too often from clients how frustrating it is to have worked hard on something only to have their leader immediately move on to the next target or goal without any kind of pause, acknowledgment, or celebration of what's just been accomplished. So much of the anxiety and insecurity I hear about seems to come from leaders who don't listen, say thank you, or acknowledge when others have gone the extra mile.

To counter this unhealthy habit, consider making it a priority to acknowledge and appreciate your employees—and to take victory laps with them when the team has completed a major initiative. Taking time to express gratitude and cultivate some team spirit can be hugely beneficial in bringing out the Leader A in all team members, and it's made for a more cohesive, productive team.

One leader kept a giant visual of a soccer field up on his office wall. On the field he listed the top three initiatives for the year, and each time the team made progress, they moved the "ball" up the field together at a team meeting. It was a vivid and concrete way of celebrating the milestones they'd achieved. Another client dedicated the first thirty minutes of every monthly staff meeting to having his team leaders share something their team accomplished or that they were especially proud of. Three benefits emerged: staff meetings started with a positive tone and energy; employees shared that it helped them to feel part of something larger than their individual silos; and they gained important information about what other areas were doing, which in turn enhanced their own objectives.

#4: Keep Purpose at the Forefront

Part of being a leader is being able to see a vision and a higher aspiration for your organization or industry and connecting that to a vision and higher aspiration you hold for those who work for you. It's about being able to see what's *possible* for the organization and for its individual employees.

Make it part of your mandate to help others become the next best version of themselves. And part of accomplishing that work requires helping people stay connected to their ever-evolving sense of purpose. As we discussed in chapter 2, one's purpose—what we are passionate about and the difference we hope to make next— changes over time. So be a leader who helps others stay connected to their dynamic sense of purpose.

It's so easy for every interaction with your direct reports to turn into a rushed conversation that's focused on getting things done, fixing problems, or putting out fires. Instead, make sure that some portion of your time together explores what drives their intrinsic motivation on the job. To do that, ask questions such as the following during natural points in the workflow:

- IN ADVANCE OF NEW EXPERIENCES: What are you excited about for this upcoming project or initiative? What are ways you hope to develop, learn, or grow with this experience?

- AFTER KEY MILESTONES: What's something you felt great about or were especially proud of on that team or project? What was especially rewarding, meaningful, or inspiring coming out of that project, initiative, or event?

- AT ANNUAL PERFORMANCE REVIEWS: What did you most enjoy working on this past year and why? What are the types of things you'd like to get more experience in for the coming year?

- IN CAREER-DEVELOPMENT CONVERSATIONS: What is your career aspiration over the next three to five years? How do you see this role helping you get there? What inspires you now?[12]

Infuse All Levels with Purpose: Individual, Team, and Organization. So far, we've discussed ways to keep purpose alive at the individual direct report level, but purpose is something to keep in mind at the team and organizational level as well. Consider the remarkable turnaround of DTE Energy as described by business professors Robert E. Quinn and Anjan V. Thakor in a *Harvard Business Review* article. After the Great Recession of 2008, DTE president Gerry Anderson knew he had to do something different to get employees more engaged and committed. He reached out to board member Joe Robles, who at that time was also the CEO of USAA. Robles invited Anderson to visit some USAA call centers, where Anderson fully expected to find bored workers just going through the motions. Instead, he found the kind of workforce he wanted at DTE: "positive, fully engaged employees [who would] collaborate and go the extra mile for customers." How had USAA achieved this? Robles's answer was simple: "a leader's most important job is 'to connect the people to their purpose.'"[13]

Anderson went back to DTE with a plan. He had a video made that articulated the employees' purpose by featuring workers describing the impact of their work on the well-being of their community. It was so effective its test audience gave it a standing ovation, and later audiences were moved to tears. Making this connection to purpose was the missing piece. "Never before," write Quinn and Thakor, "had their work been framed as a meaningful contribution to the greater good." But the video—and the salient connection it made—was just the first step. From there, DTE's leadership dedicated themselves to supporting the company's purpose, weaving it into onboarding and training programs, meetings, and culture-building activities beyond the workplace. Soon enough, nothing short of a transformation occurred. Employee engagement scores rose, DTE received a Gallup Great Workplace Award five years in a row, and from 2008 to 2017, their stock price tripled.[14]

A Final Vision and Call to Action

Leader A is not the part of you led by fear, greed, ego, scarcity, or insecurity. Nor is it your idealized superman or superwoman self who puts on a mask of strength and ability, or the person who needs to be seen as the good guy or gal, or the competent one, or the perfect one.

Leader A is the part of you that is deeply led by your character and your principles, by what you know to be right and effective for the situation at hand. It requires continuous self-awareness and self-care. It's about looking honestly at the totality of your life—your work, your home life, your leisure time, and your interests and passions in both the personal and professional arenas—and discerning the particular mix that makes you the most effective, satisfied, and fulfilled leader. Leading from a Leader A mindset never pits work against life. Arianna Huffington, author of *Thrive* and the founder of Thrive Global, said it best: "Work and life, well-being and productivity, are not on opposite sides—so they don't need to be balanced. They're on the same side, and rise in tandem."[15]

At the outset of this book, I expressed my hope that you read it as if we were in a coaching session together. Though I will never know most of you, I have been acutely aware of your presence throughout the process of writing, and I am grateful for the time you've invested here. And, like the engagements I have with my clients, as we approach the end of our time together, it feels bittersweet.

For each person I have the opportunity to ride alongside, as we have done in this book together, I leave with the same hope: that you continue to have ambition for a rich and full life, for living and leading with your highest and best, and that you continue to come to understand the conditions, people, and contexts that drive and support your own personal version of Leader A. And that you will go on to help others do the same.

Though you will likely enjoy many individual successes, good leadership isn't motivated by self-serving means. Rather, leadership practiced well constitutes a mutual dance between self and others, between our personal aspirations as leaders and our organization's goals, and between looking inward with a keen, honest eye and looking outward with an eye to progress.

Imagine a world in which leaders are operating from the calm, focused still point of their spectator self while simultaneously engaged deeply in the action. Imagine a world in which leaders deliver or even exceed the results their organizations need and continually grow into the best leaders they can be, exceeding their own expectations. And imagine a world in which leaders help others infuse purpose into their days, encourage processes and self-care practices that sustain the whole person, and bring a centered, peaceful, and effective presence to their organizations.

This is what I have imagined, and it's what I've seen is possible while working with leaders every day, out in the trenches. Now it's your turn. I am asking you to be part of the movement to develop more Leader A leaders, teams, and organizations. Start with yourself. The more you feed Leader A, the more you can count on your ripple effect to support and inspire others. And the more you live and lead from a Leader A mindset, the more you are able to help others find and feed their own version of Leader A.

Today's leaders really do face a plethora of unprecedented challenges, from the demands of our 24-7 work culture and the dizzying speed of technological advances to the inner pressures we place on ourselves. Being out front and responsible for so much—results and deliverables, team inspiration and collaboration, setting goals and agendas, bringing an organization's vision to life and making sure it's realized, and being aware of your ripple effect, not to mention cultivating the deep self-awareness required for effective leadership—is an enormous undertaking, to say the least.

But leadership is a noble calling. If practiced well, it is a calling that offers great intangible rewards that begin with the self but proliferate outward, sometimes in ways we could never have imagined. When you're living and leading from a Leader A mindset, when you and your team are bringing your Leader A game to the table and delivering superior results that make a difference in the world, you are living the life of a servant leader who, with every action, is paying it forward. There are few things in life more rewarding. This is the pinnacle not only of leadership, but of living.

The Leader A Toolkit

The Leader A
Master Checklist Tool

You can more proactively sustain being in Leader A mode or help coach others to do the same by identifying specific opportunities using the following checklist.

Leader A Checklist for Purpose (Chapter 2)

Use the "Purpose = Contribution + Passion" Equation

- ☐ Define the tangibles and intangibles of your contribution in your role now

- ☐ Look at what stokes your fire

- ☐ Recognize that purpose is ever-evolving and dynamic

Use the Purpose Quadrants to Manage Time and Energy

- ☐ Plot your contributions and passions into the purpose quadrants

- ☐ Use the purpose quadrants to prioritize, tolerate, elevate, or delegate

Use the Purpose Quadrants to Manage Transitions in Your Career

- ☐ Watch out for the boredom signals in Quadrant II

- ☐ Watch out for the misalignment signals in Quadrant III

Use Purpose for Sifting Everyday Demands and Requests

- ☐ Determine if a meeting or an extracurricular adds value to you or if you uniquely add value to it before saying yes

- ☐ Organize "yes" into three buckets: the strategic yes, the partial yes, and the "it's not actually my yes"

☐ Watch out for losing time and energy when overpackaging on presentations, overengineering a process, or staying in the weeds on any piece of work

Leader A Checklist for Process (Chapter 3)

Design Processes That Fit You and Your Context

☐ Determine where you fall on the "structured-unstructured" continuum

☐ Assess whether your natural energy flow is a "steady-as-she-goes" pace or that of a "burst tasker"

☐ Match your work activities to your chronotype to match when your energy is highest in the day

Preserve Your Time for What Matters Most

☐ Use color coding in your calendar to match the four quadrants of the passion-contribution matrix in chapter 2 and look at patterns and trend lines

☐ Set power hours

☐ Determine your time zones and home zones for work at home

☐ Employ look-aheads

☐ Make the most of white space—productively and restoratively

☐ Use the brush your teeth practice

Recharge and Restore Your Energy

☐ Employ the midweek gas tank fill-up ritual

☐ Try massage or other bodywork modalities

☐ Stretch anytime, anywhere

- ☐ Increase your sense of freedom through movement, sport, and exercise

Choose Your Top One or Two Processes

- ☐ Reframe process as a commitment to yourself, your purpose, and the vision you hope to achieve

- ☐ Use process as a way to get back on track quickly after falling into Leader B mode

- ☐ Experiment and boil it down to your top one or two must-have processes that have the most impact on your effectiveness, presence, and satisfaction

Leader A Checklist for People (Chapter 4)

Raise Your Game, Raise the Game of Others

- ☐ Adopt a mindset of making yourself obsolete with a virtuous cycle of growth

- ☐ Examine the strength of your team

- ☐ Optimize the "leverage + empower + inspire" equation

Build a Strategic Network of Support

- ☐ Recognize the importance of having a network of support as your accountabilities and performance pressures rise

- ☐ Consider whether you have each of the seven roles in your life: experts, sausage makers, accountability buddies, mirrors, helicopters, cheerleaders, and safe harbors

- ☐ Be a good citizen, enlisting support with a spirit of giving rather than taking

Update Your Boundaries and Rules of Engagement

☐ Practice bringing attention to your own needs

☐ Be clear on emotional ownership and accountabilities

☐ Respond to others and incoming requests with grace

Leader A Checklist for Presence (Chapter 5)

Stay in Action Rather Than Distraction and Procrastination

☐ Work off-line during critical power hours or when you need to focus

☐ Take single steps, shifting your attention from the mountain to the molehill

☐ Give yourself fifteen minutes to get into it

☐ Stay anchored in the physical

☐ Use a grounding visualization technique

Accelerate through Vicious Cycles and Create Virtuous Ones

☐ *Spectate:* Observe yourself and see the patterns at play

☐ *Regulate:* Find the pause and don't scratch the itch

☐ *Adapt:* Create new patterns and "if-thens"

Spectate: Observe Yourself and See the Patterns at Play

☐ Understand what distinguishes self-spectating from self-awareness

☐ Build your spectating muscle with nonjudgment and self-compassion

☐ Recognize triggers and their corresponding voice track and physiological reactions

Regulate: Find the Pause and Don't Scratch the Itch

☐ Defuse the emotional charge through cognitive labeling

☐ Extend the pause point between stimulus and response

☐ Don't scratch the itch; instead, use a mantra or swing thought, breathing techniques, or mindfulness meditation

Adapt: Create New Patterns and "If-Then" Pathways to Leader A

☐ Recognize new choices

☐ Create new "if-then" pathways from old historic patterns to new desired states

☐ Increase access to "choice of voice"

Choose the Leadership Voice Most Appropriate and Effective for the Situation

☐ Keep a consistent *voice of character* by knowing the principles that guide your interactions with others

☐ Use a *voice of context* when sharing vision, presenting to executives, or setting the stage

☐ Help others to stay focused by using a *voice of clarity* to give clear direction, set goals, and make decisions

☐ Seek to understand another person's perspective with a *voice of curiosity*

☐ Increase your *voice of connection* by telling stories, acknowledging others, and making time to build rapport with others

Leader A Checklist for Peace (Chapter 6)

Use the Acronym "ACT"

- ☐ *Accept the moment:* Take constructive and effective action for what's within your control

- ☐ *Be content in the moment:* Know what's enough and bring an attitude of gratitude

- ☐ *Trust yourself and life in the moment:* You've achieved, learned, and grown, and you will again

Accept the Moment

- ☐ *Name the resistance:* What don't you accept?

- ☐ *Get honest:* What's in your control? What is out of your control?

- ☐ Let go to accept

- ☐ Accept and own all parts of yourself

Be Content in the Moment

- ☐ Keep the value of dissatisfaction

- ☐ Set an internal barometer for "what's enough"

- ☐ Add an attitude of gratitude

Trust Yourself and Life in the Moment

- ☐ Get updated to who you are as a leader now

- ☐ Engage in a Chapters Review

- ☐ Remember who you are

- ☐ See the "so what" in everything

Transition from Striving to Greater Meaning and Purpose

- ☐ Remember the leader at peace mantra: "Let me have the humility to know what's enough, the gratitude to see that it's all enough, and the peace within to know that I am enough."

- ☐ Give yourself permission to thrive

- ☐ Have principles drive leadership action

- ☐ Accept and practice the ultimate paradox: honor self to transcend self

Leader A Checklist for Pay It Forward (Chapter 7)

Don't Underestimate Your Ripple Effect

- ☐ Recognize the impact you have on others depending on whether you are in Leader A or Leader B mode

- ☐ Choose to create a positive legacy

- ☐ Have a guiding question: "Am I choosing to be . . . a role model for others today? An agent of change who has improved the lives of others? A visionary who keeps the whole team on course?"

Develop Leader A Leaders, Teams, and Organizations

- ☐ Create a shared language using "Leader A" and "Leader B" with your teams

- ☐ Don't normalize Leader B; get to the root cause and build action plans using the five Ps

- ☐ Be a good steward of organizational time, energy, and resources

Keep Purpose at the Forefront for Teams and Organizations

- ☐ Make sure to spend time with your direct reports to explore what drives their intrinsic motivation on the job

- ☐ Connect people to the organization's purpose by articulating how day-to-day work affects vision, weaving it into on-boarding and training programs, and creating culture-building activities

The Leader A Assessment

You can more precisely identify opportunities for sustaining Leader A by taking the following assessment. Leader A and Leader B sit on a continuum and a slippery slope, so it is good to regularly lift out of the noise to see if one of your five Ps may need some additional attention. Take note of places where you marked yourself below a 5.

	1 2 3 4 5 6 7 8 9 10		
	Leader B ←————————————————→ Leader A		
	Leader B mode	**Leader A mode**	**Self-rating**
Purpose	Feels drained by work and current activities.	Is engaged in work that provides a sense of passion and contribution. Makes effective choices on yeses and nos.	_____
Process	Has become lax about structures or rituals whereby time gets eaten away and energy is drained.	Has structures and rituals that match natural energy flows, protect time, and re-store energy.	_____
People	Has weak links on the team, gets overly in-volved, lacks a net-work of support, or has poor boundaries with others.	Regularly looks at the strength of the team and has the right people on the bus. Has a strong network of support and healthy boundaries with others.	_____
Presence	Is easily triggered and readily "scratches the itch" when operating from autopilot or habit.	Is conscious and in-tentional. Is able to make effective choices for the situa-tion at hand.	_____
Peace	Feels anxious, agi-tated, or worried. Leadership actions stem from a place of striving, deficit, or the need to prove oneself.	Is at peace within and is able to accept, feel gratitude, and trust. Leadership actions stem from a place of principles and meaning.	_____

The Leader A Onboarding Worksheet Tool

If you are taking on a new role, you can more proactively ensure success by using the five Ps to see where you may need to shift or expand your capacity. Use the worksheet below for active planning. You can also use this worksheet to help someone else who may be onboarding into a new role that will impact their time and energy.

1. *What is your new role or initiative?*

_____

_____

2. *Purpose: Reset Your Compass.* What is your highest and best use in this new role? What are you most passionate and excited about for this new role?

_____

_____

3. *Process: Reboot Your Personal Operating System.* What structures or processes will you need to update in order to protect your time or recharge your energy in this role?

_____

_____

4. *People: Raise Your Game, Raise the Game of Others.* What will you need to do differently to leverage, empower, and inspire your team in this new role? What network of support do you need to be successful now? What updates to boundaries or rules of engagement with others will you need to navigate or establish?

———————————————————————————————

———————————————————————————————

5. *Presence: Don't Scratch the Itch*. What old habits or triggers could get in the way of your success in this new role? What are new habits you would like to put in place to ensure success in this new role?

———————————————————————————————

———————————————————————————————

6. *Peace: Loosen the Grip*. What leadership principles and values will be important to guiding you in this new role? What milestones will you celebrate along the way?

———————————————————————————————

———————————————————————————————

Managing Overwork or Stress Worksheet Tool

If you are in a period of overwork or stress, you can more proactively get back to Leader A mode by using the five Ps *in reverse order*. You can also use this worksheet to help someone else who may be experiencing overwork or stress at this time as well.

1. *What is the current situation or context you're struggling with?*

_____

_____

2. *Peace: Loosen the Grip.* Where do you feel the most resistance at this time? What is within your control and what is outside your control?

_____

_____

3. *Presence: Don't Scratch the Itch.* How can you bring yourself some self-compassion at this time? What mantra or mindfulness technique can you use to regain your sense of agency, control, or choice?

_____

_____

4. *People: Raise Your Game, Raise the Game of Others.* Who can you reach out to for help, for a fresh perspective, or to delegate to? Who might you need to say no to or renegotiate a deadline with?

_____

_____

5. Process: Reboot Your Personal Operating System. What is a key process, structure, or ritual you can use or reemploy to regain your sense of agency, control, or choice?

_____

_____

6. Purpose: Reset the Compass. What do you need to reprioritize right now? What are your strategic yesses and nos right now?

_____

_____

Increasing Effectiveness, Discipline, Collaboration, or Satisfaction Tool

If you are looking to improve your effectiveness, discipline, collaboration, or satisfaction on the job, you can target specific Ps and use them in combination. You can also use this tool if you are a coach or leader helping someone improve in any of these areas. The graphic and instructions below give you a guide for where to direct your actions.

1. If you want to increase your overall *effectiveness at work*, then look for the opportunities in *purpose + process + people*.

2. If you want to increase your ability to *collaborate with others*, then look for opportunities in *purpose + people + peace*.

FIGURE A-1

Use the Ps in combination

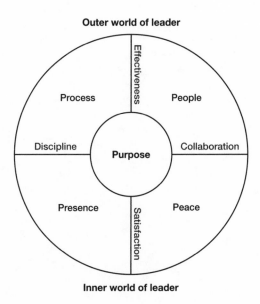

3. If you want to increase your *overall discipline*, then look for opportunities in *purpose + process + presence*.

4. If you want to increase your overall *sense of satisfaction in work and life,* then look for opportunities in *purpose + presence + peace.*

NOTES

INTRODUCTION

1. Emma Seppälä and Julia Moeller, "1 in 5 Employees Is Highly Engaged and at Risk of Burnout," February 2, 2018, https://hbr.org/2018/02/1-in-5-highly -engaged-employees-is-at-risk-of-burnout; Rob Cross, Reb Rebele, and Adam M. Grant, "Collaborative Overload," *Harvard Business Review*, January– February 2016, 74–79.

2. Jen Fisher, "How Managers Can Prevent Their Teams from Burning Out," July 31, 2018, https://hbr.org/2018/07/how-managers-can-prevent-their-teams -from-burning-out.

3. Betty Hung, email exchange with author, March 30, 2017.

4. Thomas Hellwig, Caroline Rook, Elizabeth Florent-Treacy, and Man- fred F. R. Kets de Vries, "An Early Warning System for Your Team's Stress Level," https://hbr.org/2017/04/an-early-warning-system-for-your-teams-stress-level.

5. Eric Garton, "Employee Burnout Is a Problem with the Company, Not the Person," April 6, 2017, https://hbr.org/2017/04/employee-burnout-is-a-problem -with-the-company-not-the-person.

6. Ron Carucci, "The Better You Know Yourself, the More Resilient You'll Be," September 4, 2017, https://hbr.org/2017/09/the-better-you-know-yourself -the-more-resilient-youll-be.

7. "Poiesis," Wikipedia, January 3, 2019, https://en.wikipedia.org/wiki /Poiesis.

8. Norman Fischer, "The One Who Is Not Busy," *O Magazine*, September 2008.

9. Justin Bariso, "It Took LinkedIn's CEO Exactly 2 Sentences to Give the Best Career Advice You'll Hear Today," *Inc.*, September 20, 2017, https://www .inc.com/justin-bariso/it-took-linkedins-ceo-exactly-2-sentences-to-give-.html? _lrsc=52ca5426-9388-4d18-a9e6-c1e571d48aac.

10. OWN SuperSoul Sunday, "Interview with Jeff Weiner—Five Keys to Happiness that LinkedIn CEO Jeff Weiner Lives By," YouTube video, 1:47, September 18, 2018, https://www.youtube.com/watch?v=g1W1vRE4tU8.

CHAPTER ONE

1. Laura Empson, "If You're So Successful, Why Are You Still Working 70 Hours a Week?" February 1, 2018, https://hbr.org/2018/02/if-youre-so-successful -why-are-you-still-working-70-hours-a-week.

2. Greg McKeown, "Why We Humblebrag About Being Busy," June 6, 2014, https://hbr.org/2014/06/why-we-humblebrag-about-being-busy.

CHAPTER TWO

1. John Hagel, Alok Ranjan, John Seely Brown, and Daniel Byler, "Passion at Work: Cultivating Worker Passion as a Cornerstone of Talent Development," *Deloitte Insights*, October 7, 2014, https://www2.deloitte.com/insights/us/en /topics/talent/worker-passion-employee-behavior.html.

2. Scott Barry Kaufman, "Why Inspiration Matters," November 8, 2011, https://hbr.org/2011/11/why-inspiration-matters.

3. "Mark Zuckerberg's Commencement Address at Harvard," *The Harvard Gazette,* https://news.harvard.edu/gazette/story/2017/05/mark-zuckerbergs -speech-as-written-for-harvards-class-of-2017.

4. Beth Kowitt, "Ex-Lululemon CEO on Why She Left the Company," *Fortune*, December 3, 2014, http://fortune.com/2014/12/03/lululemon-ceo/.

CHAPTER THREE

1. Michaéla C. Schippers and Paul A. M. Van Lange, "The Psychological Benefits of Superstitious Rituals in Top Sport: A Study Among Top Sportsmen," *Journal of Applied Social Psychology*, 36 (2006): 2532–2553. http://citeseerx.ist.psu.edu/viewdoc/download?doi=10.1.1.314.2165&rep =rep1&type=pdf.

2. Christopher M. Barnes, "The Ideal Work Schedule, as Determined by Circadian Rhythms," January 28, 2015, https://hbr.org/2015/01/the-ideal-work -schedule-as-determined-by-circadian-rhythms.

3. Ibid.

4. Ibid.

5. Jim Loehr and Tony Schwartz, *The Power of Full Engagement: Managing Energy, Not Time, Is the Key to High Performance and Personal Renewal* (New York: Free Press, 2003), 31.

6. Kristen Duke, Adrian Ward, Ayelet Gneezy, and Maarten Bos, "Having Your Smartphone Nearby Takes a Toll on Your Thinking," March 20, 2018, https://hbr.org/2018/03/having-your-smartphone-nearby-takes-a-toll-on-your -thinking.

7. Anna Hensel, "How This Co-Founder of a $4 Billion Company Works Only 7 Hours a Day," *Inc.*, April 2017, https://www.inc.com/magazine/201704 /anna-hensel/day-in-the-life-cal-henderson.html.

8. Shawn Achor and Michelle Gielan, "Resilience Is About How You Recharge, Not How You Endure," June 24, 2016, https://hbr.org/2016/06 /resilience-is-about-how-you-recharge-not-how-you-endure.

9. American Academy of Sleep Medicine, "Insomnia Costing US Workforce $63.2 Billion a Year in Lost Productivity, Study Shows," *ScienceDaily*, September 2, 2011, www.sciencedaily.com/releases/2011/09/110901093653.htm.

10. Ibid.

11. Mayo Clinic, "Massage: Get in Touch With Its Many Benefits," October 6, 2018, https://www.mayoclinic.org/healthy-lifestyle/stress-management/in -depth/massage/art-20045743.

12. Tim Newman, "Everything You Need to Know About Reiki," *Medical News Today*, September 6, 2017, https://www.medicalnewstoday.com/articles /308772.php.

13. Harvard Medical School, "The Importance of Stretching," September 2013, https://www.health.harvard.edu/staying-healthy/the-importance-of -stretching.

14. Maria Cohut, "Aerobic Exercise: 'A Maintenance Program for the Brain,'" *Medical News Today*, November 16, 2017, https://www .medicalnewstoday.com/articles/320065.php.

15. Leo Widrich, "What Happens to Our Brains When We Exercise and How It Makes Us Happier," *Fast Company*, February 4, 2014, https://www.fastcomp any.com/3025957/what-happens-to-our-brains-when-we-exercise-and-how-it -makes-us-happier.

16. Ibid.

17. Andrew Rundle, "Just How Bad Is Business Travel for Your Health? Here's the Data," May 31, 2018, https://hbr.org/2018/05/just-how-bad-is -business-travel-for-your-health-heres-the-data.

18. Hensel, "How This Co-Founder of a $4 Billion Company Works Only 7 Hours a Day."

CHAPTER FOUR

1. Adam Grant, "In the Company of Givers and Takers," *Harvard Business Review*, April 2013, 90–97.

2. OWN SuperSoul Sunday, "Interview with Jeff Weiner—The Most Important Lesson Jeff Weiner Learned as the CEO of LinkedIn," YouTube video, 3:18, September 16, 2018, https://www.youtube.com/watch?v=S -QNwKiu5xU.

3. Morten T. Hansen and Bolko von Oetinger, "Introducing T-Shaped Managers, Knowledge Management's Next Generation, *Harvard Business Review*, March 2001, 106–116.

4. Michael J. Socolow, "Rowing's Search for Swing," *Boston Globe*, October 23, 2016, https://www.bostonglobe.com/ideas/2016/10/22/rowing-search-for -swing/atZLkSvjEr05fp2d2Tg30J/story.html.

5. Ibid.

6. Peter Dean, "Business Leaders: Row All in the Same Boat," *Wharton Magazine*, September 18, 2014, http://whartonmagazine.com/blogs/business -leaders-row-all-in-the-same-boat/#sthash.jBK4gfJN.5HLFQFmC.dpbs.

7. Alina Tugend, "Why Is Asking for Help So Difficult?" *New York Times*, July 7, 2007, http://www.nytimes.com/2007/07/07/business/07shortcuts.html.

8. Wayne Baker, "5 Ways to Get Better at Asking for Help," December 18, 2014, https://hbr.org/2014/12/5-ways-to-get-better-at-asking-for-help.

9. Laura Hilgers, "Wise Eyes, Fresh Eyes," *Southwest: The Magazine*, January 2019, https://www.southwestmag.com/chip-conley/.

10. Ibid.

11. Shunryu Suzuki, *Zen Mind, Beginner's Mind: Informal Talks on Zen Meditation and Practice* (Boulder, CO: Shambhala, 2011).

12. Amy C. Edmondson, "The Competitive Imperative of Learning," *Harvard Business Review*, July–August 2008, 60–67.

13. Grant, "In the Company of Givers and Takers."

14. Ibid.

15. Charles Duhigg, "What Google Learned from Its Quest to Build the Perfect Team," *New York Times*, February 25, 2016, https://www.nytimes.com/2016/02/28/magazine/what-google-learned-from-its-quest-to-build-the-perfect-team.html.

CHAPTER FIVE

1. Nicole Torres, "Just Hearing Your Phone Buzz Hurts Your Productivity," July 10, 2015, https://hbr.org/2015/07/just-hearing-your-phone-buzz-hurts-your-productivity.

2. Rasmus Hougaard and Jacqueline Carter, "If You Aspire to Be a Great Leader, Be Present," December 13, 2017, https://hbr.org/2017/12/if-you-aspire-to-be-a-great-leader-be-present.

3. Jon Kabat-Zinn, *Full Catastrophe Living* (New York: Bantam, 2013).

4. Robert Kegan and Lisa Laskow Lahey, *Immunity to Change: How to Overcome It and Unlock the Potential in Yourself and Your Organization* (Boston: Harvard Business Review Press, 2009).

5. Ibid.

6. Ronald Heifetz and Marty Linsky, "A Survival Guide for Leaders," *Harvard Business Review*, June 2002, 65–74.

7. Anne Grady, "Handle Your Stress Better by Knowing What Causes It," June 21, 2017, https://hbr.org/2017/06/handle-your-stress-better-by-knowing-what-causes-it.

8. David Rock, "SCARF: A Brain-Based Model for Collaborating with and Influencing Others," *NeuroLeadership Journal* 1, no. 1 (2008).

9. Charlotte Lieberman, "Why You Should Stop Being So Hard on Yourself," *New York Times*, May 22, 2018, https://mobile.nytimes.com/2018/05/22/smarter-living/why-you-should-stop-being-so-hard-on-yourself.html?smid=fb-nytimes&smtyp=cur.

10. Rock, "SCARF."

11. Amy Jen Su, "5 Ways to Focus Your Energy During a Work Crunch," September 22, 2017, https://hbr.org/2017/09/5-ways-to-focus-your-energy-during-a-work-crunch.

12. Susan David, "3 Ways to Better Understand Your Emotions," November 10, 2016, https://hbr.org/2016/11/3-ways-to-better-understand-your-emotions; Todd B. Kashdan, Lisa Feldman Barrett, Patrick E. McKnight, "Unpacking Emotion Differentiation: Transforming Unpleasant Experience by Perceiving Distinctions in Negativity," *Current Directions in Psychological Science* 24, no. 1 (2015): 10–16.

13. Chade-Meng Tan, *Search Inside Yourself: The Unexpected Guide to Achieving Success, Happiness (& World Peace)* (San Francisco: HarperOne, 2014), 119.

14. Kris Nimsger, email exchange with author, May 31, 2018.

15. Tris Thorp, "What Is a Mantra?" The Chopra Center, https://chopra.com /articles/what-is-a-mantra.

16. "Golf Swing Thought—To Think or Not, That Is the Question," The Barefoot Golfer, May 28, 2013, http://www.thebarefootgolfer.com/swing-thought -to-think-or-not-that-is-the-question/.

17. "4-7-8 Breathing: Health Benefits and Demonstration," Dr. Weil video, 8:16, https://www.drweil.com/videos-features/videos/the-4-7-8-breath-health -benefits-demonstration/.

18. Amishi Jha, "The Science of Taming the Wandering Mind," *Mindful*, June 16, 2017, https://www.mindful.org/taming-the-wandering-mind/.

19. Rich Fernandez, "Help Your Team Manage Stress, Anxiety, and Burnout," January 21, 2016, https://hbr.org/2016/01/help-your-team-manage-stress-anxiety -and-burnout.

20. Jha, "The Science of Taming the Wandering Mind."

21. Heidi Grant, "Get Your Team to Do What It Says It's Going to Do," *Harvard Business Review*, May 2014, 82–87.

CHAPTER SIX

1. Oxford dictionary contributors, "resistance," *English Oxford Living Dictionaries,* https://en.oxforddictionaries.com/definition/resistance.

2. "Electrical Resistance and Conductance," Wikipedia, June 30, 2019, https://en.wikipedia.org/w/index.php?title=Electrical_resistance_and _conductance&oldid=887883815.

3. Brené Brown, *Dare to Lead: Brave Work. Tough Conversations. Whole Hearts* (New York: Random House, 2018).

4. Sean Gregory, "Serena Williams Opens Up About Her Complicated Comeback, Motherhood and Taking Time to Be Selfish," *Time*, August 16, 2018, http://time.com/5368858/serena-williams-comeback/.

5. Ibid.

6. Stephen Blyth, "Cancer, Chemo, and the Road to Self-Compassion," *Boston Globe*, October 10, 2017, https://www.bostonglobe.com/opinion/2017/10/09/cancer -chemo-and-road-self-compassion/27h4g3idTBd4qF9OLUjZ1L/story.html.

7. Ibid.

8. David DeSteno, "Gratitude Is the New Willpower," April 9, 2014, https:// hbr.org/2014/04/gratitude-is-the-new-willpower.

9. David DeSteno, "How to Cultivate Gratitude, Compassion, and Pride on Your Team," February 20, 2018, https://hbr.org/2018/02/how-to-cultivate -gratitude-compassion-and-pride-on-your-team.

10. Jessica Stillman, "Gratitude Physically Changes Your Brain, New Study Says," *Inc.*, January 15, 2016, https://www.inc.com/jessica-stillman/the-amazing -way-gratitude-rewires-your-brain-for-happiness.html.

11. Shawn Achor, "Positive Intelligence," *Harvard Business Review*, January–February 2012, 100–109.

12. Alan Morinis, *Everyday Holiness: The Jewish Spiritual Path of Mussar* (Boston: Trumpeter, 2008).

13. Bill George, "HBS: The Truth About Authentic Leaders," Bill George, July 6, 2016, http://www.billgeorge.org/articles/hbs-the-truth-about-authentic-leaders/.

14. Mary Oliver, "Wild Geese," *Dream Work* (New York: Atlantic Monthly Press, 1986).

15. Ikujiro Nonaka and Hirotaka Takeuchi, "The Big Idea: The Wise Leader," *Harvard Business Review*, May 2011, 58–67.

16. David Rooke and William R. Torbert, "Seven Transformations of Leadership," *Harvard Business Review*, April 2005, 66–76.

17. Ibid.

18. Jim Collins and Morten T. Hansen, "Level 5 Leadership and 10x Entrepreneurial Success," Jim Collins, https://www.jimcollins.com/article_topics/articles/level-5-leadership.html.

19. Jenna Goudreau, "7 Surprising Ways to Motivate Millennial Workers," *Forbes*, March 7, 2013, https://www.forbes.com/sites/jennagoudreau/2013/03/07/7-surprising-ways-to-motivate-millennial-workers/.

20. Eric Garton and Michael Mankins, "Engaging Your Employees Is Good, but Don't Stop There," December 9, 2015, https://hbr.org/2015/12/engaging-your-employees-is-good-but-dont-stop-there.

21. Catherine Bailey and Adrian Madden, "What Makes Work Meaningful—Or Meaningless," *MIT Sloan Management Review*, Summer 2016, https://sloanreview.mit.edu/article/what-makes-work-meaningful-or-meaningless/.

CHAPTER SEVEN

1. Amy Jen Su, "How to Help Someone Find Work That Excites Them," September 13, 2017, https://hbr.org/2017/09/how-to-help-someone-discover-work-that-excites-them.

2. Amy Jen Su and Muriel Maignan Wilkins, "What's Your Ripple Effect?," *Leader to Leader Magazine*, March 17, 2014, https://doi.org/10.1002/ltl.20127.

3. Jennifer Robison, "Well-Being Is Contagious (For Better or Worse)," *Business Journal*, November 27, 2012, https://news.gallup.com/businessjournal/158732/wellbeing-contagious-better-worse.aspx.

4. Clayton M. Christensen, "How Will You Measure Your Life?" *Harvard Business Review*, July–August 2010, 46–51.

5. Christine Porath, *Mastering Civility: A Manifesto for the Workplace* (New York: Grand Central Publishing, 2016).

6. Heike Bruch and Jochen I. Menges, "The Acceleration Trap," *Harvard Business Review*, April 2010, 80–86.

7. Diana Kander, "Help Your Team Stop Overcommitting by Empowering Them to Say No," June 6, 2017, https://hbr.org/2017/06/help-your-team-stop-overcommitting-by-empowering-them-to-say-no.

8. Ibid.

9. Bruch and Menges, "The Acceleration Trap."

10. Maura Thomas, "Your Late-Night Emails Are Hurting Your Team," March 16, 2015, https://hbr.org/2015/03/your-late-night-emails-are-hurting-your -team.

11. David Gelles, "At Aetna, a C.E.O.'s Management by Mantra," *New York Times*, February 27, 2015, https://www.nytimes.com/2015/03/01/business/at -aetna-a-ceos-management-by-mantra.html?_r=0.

12. Su, "How to Help Someone Find Work That Excites Them."

13. Robert E. Quinn and Anjan V. Thakor, "Creating a Purpose-Driven Organization," *Harvard Business Review*, July–August 2018, 78–85.

14. Ibid.

15. Arianna Huffington, "From Ariana Huffington: Welcome to Thrive Global," *Medium*, November 30, 2016, https://medium.com/thrive-global /arianna-huffington-welcome-to-thrive-global-bbdaea4aa455.

INDEX

acceptance
  embrace parts of self for, 166–167
  honesty and, 162–163
  resistance and, 160–162
  step for peace, 160–167, 186
  transitions and change stages with, 163–166
  truth-seeking and, 167
accountability buddies, 110, 113, 123, 210
Achor, Shawn, 173
acknowledgment, 108, 111–112, 114, 120–121, 153, 201, 212
Adaptive Leadership (Heifetz and Linsky), 132
adapt step in virtuous cycles, 145–149
Advantage, The (Lencioni), 80–81
Aetna, 210
alchemists, 184–185
Anderson, Gerry, 203

Baker, Wayne, 107
Barnes, Christopher M., 65
beginner's mind, 108–109
Bertolini, Mark, 210
Bhagavad Gita, 40–41
blood circulation, 89
Blyth, Stephen, 172
boredom, 51, 58, 182, 208
Boston Globe, 172
boundaries for people, 124
  attention to self needs, 116–117
  continuum for, 120
  emotional ownership and accountability with, 118–122
  in responses, 120–122
  values and fears in, 118–119
Brady, Tom, 60–62

brain-derived neurotrophic factor (BDNF), 86
breathing, 140–141
Brown, Brené, 163
Bruch, Heike, 199–200
brushing teeth practice, 78–80, 90, 127
Buddhism, 60–61, 109, 144, 149, 168–169
burnout, 4–5, 12, 23, 47, 194, 201
burst taskers, 64, 66–67, 86, 91, 197, 209

Carucci, Ron, 5
Chapters Review, 176–180
character, 150, 153, 156, 204, 212
cheerleaders, 111–112, 123, 146, 210
Chesky, Brian, 109
chronotypes, 65, 91, 209
circadian rhythms, 64–65, 91
clarity, 14, 24, 53, 110, 151, 156, 212
clean-up meditation, 144–145
cognitive labeling, 138, 212
Collins, Jim, 184–185
color coding
  of calendar, 86, 91, 102, 209
  of quadrants, 45, 68–71
compass, 35, 57, 182–183, 217, 220
conductance, 162
conformity, 40–41
Conley, Chip, 109
contacts management, 75
contentment
  dissatisfaction and, 170
  internal barometer and, 171–172
  step for peace, 167–174, 186
context
  leadership voice of, 150–151
  process and, 62–68

contribution
  purpose = contribution + passion
    equation, 36–42, 208
  tangible and intangible elements,
    36–38
contribution-passion filter, 39, 209
  requests and, 53–56, 58
  work products and, 56
coping mechanisms, 13, 20, 104, 139,
  146
cranial sacral therapy, 84
curiosity, 7, 151–152, 156, 212

Dare to Lead (Brown), 163
David, Susan, 139
Dean, Peter, 106
decision-making, 18, 100–101, 151,
  199–200
delegate, hire, or eliminate quadrant,
  47–48
deliverables, 26, 37, 64, 66, 171, 205
Deloitte study, 4, 38
dharma, 40–41
dissatisfaction, 3, 127, 167, 170, 213
DTE Energy, 203–204
duty, 40–41, 98–99

Edmondson, Amy, 112, 114
Effectiveness, Discipline, Collaboration,
  Satisfaction tool, 221–222
elevate quadrant, 46–47
email management, 75
Emotional Agility (David), 139
emotional charge, 138–139, 212
emotional ownership (EO), 118–122,
  211
emotional quotient (EQ), 119, 121
empowerment, 100–104, 199
  See also leverage + empower +
    inspire equation
energy flow
  exercise for, 67–68
  for Leader A mode, 63–64
  for self-care, 65–67
  times of, 64–65
equanimity, 10, 14, 159, 168

Essentialism (McKeown), 22–23
Everyday Holiness (Morinis),
  173–174
executive assistants (EAs), 102–103
exercise, 85–87
experts, 37, 78, 108–109, 123, 210

Federer, Roger, 61
Fernandez, Rich, 142
First 20 Minutes, The (Reynolds),
  86–87
five Ps
  action plan with, 214
  alignment with, 168
  framework for, 9
  increasing effectiveness, discipline,
    collaboration, or satisfaction tool,
    221–222
  for Leader A mode, 7–10, 14,
    30–32, 196–197
  onboarding worksheet tool,
    217–219
  overwork or stress worksheet tool,
    219–220
  role of, 12
  See also peace; people; presence;
    process; purpose
focus
  fifteen minutes for, 128, 155
  grounded visualization for, 129, 155
  off-line work for, 128, 155
  physical anchoring for, 129, 155
  for presence, 127–129, 155, 183
  single steps for, 128, 155
free-thinking time, 78–79
Furl, Brent, 82

Gallico, Paul, 105
Gates, Bill, 95
generosity, 32
golden mean, 169
Gollwitzer, Peter, 148
Grady, Anne, 133
Grant, Adam, 113
gratitude, 114, 153, 160, 173–174,
  186–187

great exultation, 105
Greenleaf, Robert, 189–190
grounded visualization, 129, 155

Harvard Business Review, 198, 199,
    203
Heifetz, Ronald, 132
helicopters, 111, 113, 123, 210
help, asking for, 107–108
"Help Your Team Stop
    Overcommitting by Empowering
    Them to Say No" (Kander), 199
Henderson, Cal, 73
homeostatic value, 82
home zones, 72–75, 91, 209
honesty, 34, 162–163
hub and spoke, 104–107
Huffington, Arianna, 83, 204
humility, 32, 109, 174–175, 184, 187
Hung, Betty, 4

ice-breaking, 153
if-then tool, 130, 145, 147–149, 155,
    197, 211, 212
influence, 37–38
inner spectator, 11–12, 30, 168, 171
inspiration, 38–39, 57, 61, 104–107,
    205
    See also leverage + empower +
    inspire equation

Jha, Amishi, 141
Jobs, Steve, 78, 199
Just Do It Later Pitfall, 20, 26–27, 31,
    116, 136, 196
Just Do It Myself Pitfall, 20, 25–26,
    31, 93, 96, 104, 137, 196
Just Do It Now Pitfall, 20, 24–25, 31,
    55, 59, 196
Just Do More Pitfall, 20, 22–23,
    33–34, 55, 96, 196

Kabat-Zinn, Jon, 131
Kander, Diana, 199
Kaufman, Scott Barry, 38–39
Kegan, Bob, 131

Kornfield, Jack, 143–144, 169
Krulitz, Pam, 126

Lahey, Lisa Laskow, 131
Lao Tzu, 13, 78, 128
Leader A mode
    assessment for, 216
    benefits and rewards of, 6–7
    call to action for, 204–206
    control and, 162
    cultural norms and processes in,
        200–202
    decision-making frameworks in,
        199–200
    energy flow for, 63–64
    five Ps for, 7–10, 14, 30–32,
        196–197
    how to feed, 30–31
    lens of, 19–20, 30–32, 168–169,
        174, 179
    Master Checklist Tool for,
        208–215
    mindset, 10, 34, 57, 94–95, 104,
        165, 168, 197, 204–206
    needs and, 135
    onboarding worksheet tool,
        217–219
    operations in, 1–2
    organizational time, energy,
        resources and, 197–202
    overwork or stress worksheet tool,
        219–220
    peace and, 159
    people and, 94–95, 122–123
    perspective in, 111
    presence and, 126–127
    prioritization in, 198–199
    process and, 60–62, 90
    purpose and, 35–36, 202–204
    ripple effect in, 191–192
    rituals and, 83, 216
    shared language of, with teams,
        193–195
    shift from Leader B mode, 196
    team victory laps in, 201–202
    as whole-person approach, 8

Leader B mode
  assessment for, 216
  burnout in, 4–5
  career dissatisfaction in, 4
  challenges of, 3
  lens of, 19–20, 30–32, 164, 176
  mindset, 20, 24, 134, 138
  needs and, 135
  negative health issues in, 5
  normalization of, 195–197
  operations in, 1–2
  peace and, 159
  people and, 94–95, 123
  presence and, 126–127
  process and, 60–62, 90
  purpose and, 35–36
  resistance and, 162
  ripple effect in, 5, 190–191,
    195
  rise and costs of, 2–5
  rituals and, 216
  shared language of, with teams,
    193–195
  shift to Leader A mode, 196
  slippery slope to, 17, 21, 29, 30
  stalled careers and inability to scale
    in, 4
leadership development, 173, 181
  transcend self in, 187
  vision in, 183–184
Leadership on the Line (Heifetz and
    Linsky), 132
leadership voice
  of character, 150
  of clarity, 151
  of connection, 152–153
  of context, 150–151
  of curiosity, 151–152
  exercise, 154
  for presence, 149–154, 156
Lencioni, Patrick, 80–81
Level 5 executive, 184–185
leverage + empower + inspire equation
  capability and motivation in,
    100–104
  in home, 106
  hub and spoke and, 104–107
  for team strength, 95, 98–107
  Who Owns What in, 98–101
Linsky, Marty, 132
look-aheads, 76, 87, 91, 102, 209

mantra, 140, 148, 150, 163, 174, 212,
    214
massage, 84
Mastering Civility (Porath),
    195–196
McKeown, Greg, 22–23
meaningful work, 2, 6, 27,
    185–186
Menges, Jochen I., 199–200
middle way, 163, 168–169
midweek gas tank fill-up, 83–84, 90,
    209
mindfulness, 131, 141–142, 219
mirrors, 111, 113, 123, 210
misalignment signal, 51–52, 58, 208
Morinis, Alan, 173–174
motivation, 38, 41, 50, 57, 104,
    150, 159

network of support
  accountability buddies in, 110, 113,
    123, 210
  asking for help, 107–108
  cheerleaders in, 111–112, 123
  exercise for, 112–113
  experts in, 108–109
  give-and-take with, 113–114
  helicopters in, 111, 123
  home team as, 115
  mirrors in, 111, 123
  safe harbors in, 112, 123
  sausage makers in, 110, 123
New York Times, 86, 107
New York Times Magazine,
    113
Nimsger, Kris, 139
nonjudgment, 131, 137–138

Ohanian, Alexis, 88
Oliver, Mary, 181

onboarding worksheet tool,
217–219
overwork or stress worksheet tool,
219–220

paranoia, 175–176
passion, 4, 7
  contribution-passion filter, 39,
    53–56, 58, 209
  as fuel for action, 38–42
  purpose = contribution + passion
    equation, 36–42, 208
peace, 9, 14
  acceptance step for, 160–167, 186
  checklist tool for, 213–214
  contentment step for, 167–174, 186
  gratitude and, 173–174
  impact on Leader A and Leader B
    modes, 159
  inner confidence and strength from,
    183
  leadership from generosity, humility,
    servant leadership, 32
  overview, 156–159
  transition to greater meaning and
    purpose, 180–186
  trust step for, 174–180, 186–187
  what to remember, 186–187
Peak (Conley), 109
people, 8–9, 14
  boundaries for, 116–122, 124
  checklist tool for, 210–211
  community of support, 32
  impact on Leader A and Leader B
    modes, 94–95
  Leader A mode and, 122–123
  Leader B mode and, 123
  network of support, 107–115
  overview, 93–94
  rules-of-engagement for, 116–122,
    124
  summary, 122
  support for growth, 183
  team strength and, 95–107, 123
  what to remember, 122–124
permission to thrive, 181, 214

personal agency, 11–12
personal preferences
  for process, 63–65
  for self-care, 65–67
pitfalls of doing, 13–14
  assessment of, 28–29
  Just Do It Later Pitfall, 20, 26–27,
    31, 116, 136, 196
  Just Do It Myself Pitfall, 20, 25–26,
    31, 93, 96, 104, 137, 196
  Just Do It Now Pitfall, 20, 24–25,
    31, 55, 59, 196
  Just Do More Pitfall, 20, 22–23, 31,
    33–34, 55, 96, 196
  lens of Leader A or Leader B mode,
    19–20, 30–32
  overview, 17–19
  slippery slope to Leader B mode,
    17, 21, 29, 30
  what to remember, 32
poiesis, 7
Porath, Christine, 195–196
Post-it notes, 74–75, 90
power hours, 71–72, 78, 88, 90, 91,
    197, 209
presence, 9, 14, 32, 38
  checklist tool for, 211–212
  focus for, 127–129, 155, 183
  fully present leader, 154
  impact on Leader A and Leader B
    modes, 126–127
  leadership voice for, 149–154, 156
  overview, 125–126
  virtuous cycle creation for,
    130–149, 155
  what to remember, 155–156
prioritization, 146, 191, 208, 220
  in Leader A mode, 198–199
  prioritize quadrant, 44–45
process, 8–9, 14
  checklist tool for, 209–210
  context and, 62–68
  development of individual, 89–91
  honor rhythms and routines, 183
  impact on Leader A and Leader B
    modes, 60–62, 90

process (*continued*)
overview, 59–60
personal preferences for, 63–65
Post-it notes and technology apps for, 74–75, 90
for recharge and restoration, 81–87
rituals in, 183, 197
time management in, 68–81
travel rituals in, 87–89, 91
upgrades for, 31–32, 80–81
what to remember, 90–91
project management, 75
psychological safety, 108, 112, 114, 122
purpose, 8–9, 14
Bhagavad Gita on, 40–41
checklist tool for, 208–209
compass in, 35, 57, 182–183, 217, 220
conclusion, 56–57
connection to, 31
as dynamic and ever-evolving, 42–43
impact on Leader A and Leader B modes, 35–36
Leader A mode and, 202–204
overview, 33–35
purpose = contribution + passion equation, 36–42, 208
requests and, 208
what to remember, 57–58
purpose quadrants, 57
delegate, hire, or eliminate quadrant, 47–48
elevate quadrant, 46–47
for everyday life, 52
for management of transitions, 51–52
prioritize quadrant, 44–45
questions for setting up, 48–50
for time and energy management, 43–50
tolerate quadrant, 45–46

Quinn, Robert E., 203

Ramarajan, Lakshmi, 177
rapport building, 153, 212
recharge and restoration processes
during air flights, 88
benefits of, 81–83
midweek gas tank fill-up, 83–84, 90
passive forms of, 84
sleep as, 83–84
sports as, 85–87
stretching exercises for, 85
regulate step in virtuous cycles
defuse emotional charge, 138–139
sacred pause and, 139–145
reiki, 84
requests, 113
contribution-passion filter and, 53–56, 58
purpose and, 208
response to, 116–117, 124, 211
resistance, 160–162, 166
Reynolds, Gretchen, 86–87
right speech and right action, 149
ripple effect, 5, 190–192, 196, 205, 214
Rising to Power (Carucci), 5
rituals, 60–61
Leader A mode and, 83, 216
Leader B mode and, 216
process and, 183, 197
travel, 87–89, 91
Robles, Joe, 203
Rock, David, 134, 138
Rooke, David, 184–185
rowing, 105–106
rules-of-engagement, 116–122, 124

sacred pause, 139–145
safe harbors, 112, 113, 116, 123, 133, 146, 210
sausage makers, 110, 113, 123, 133, 210
SCARF model, 134–136
Schulz, Hans, 198–199
Search Inside Yourself (Tan), 139
self-awareness, 11, 14, 131, 171, 176–177, 191–192, 211

self-care, 11–12, 65–67, 70, 82, 116, 182, 204–205

self-compassion, 137–138, 165, 172, 174, 211, 219

servant leadership, 32, 159, 183, 187, 189, 206

Shunryu Suzuki, 109

Shuster, Loren, 129

sitting meditation, 142

sleep, 83–84

Sleep Revolution, The (Huffington), 83

smartphones, 62, 73, 90

Socolow, Michael, 105

spectator-awareness, 158
  debrief for, 133
  identify triggers for, 133–134
  muscle for, 132
  nonjudgment for, 131, 137–138
  SCARF model for, 134–136
  self-compassion for, 137–138
  subject-object capability, 131
  voice track for, 136–137
  way to step out of action, 132

sports, 85–87

storytelling, 152

subject-object capability, 131

succession planning, 97–98

sweet-spot activities, 44, 68, 69

swing, 105

swing thought, 140, 212

Tan, Chade-Meng, 139

Taoism, 10

teams
  home team, 115
  shared language with Leader A and B modes, 193–195
  team victory, 201–202

team strength, 123
  examination of, 95–96
  leverage + empower + inspire equation for, 95, 98–107
  succession planning and, 97–98

technology apps, 74–75

Thakor, Anjan V., 203

thought leadership and strategy, 37, 78

Thrive (Huffington), 204

time and energy management
  brushing teeth practice in, 78–80, 90, 127
  color coding quadrants for, 45, 68–71, 91, 209
  free-thinking time in, 78–79
  home zones and time zones in, 72–75
  look-aheads in, 76
  power hours in, 71–72
  in process, 68–81
  purpose quadrants for, 43–50
  white space in, 76–78, 83

Time magazine, 165

time zones, 72–75

tolerate quadrant, 45–46

Torbert, William, 184–185

Toyoda, Eiji, 181

transcend self, 182–187

transitions and change stages, 163–166

travel
  blood circulation during, 89
  networking time, 87–88
  productive on flight out, restore and relax on flight in, 88
  rituals, 87–89, 91
  white space during, 89

trust
  Chapters Review for, 176–180
  step for peace, 174–180, 186–187
  update as leader, 175–176

T-shaped management, 100

ultimate paradox, 182–186

virtuous cycles
  adapt step, 145–149
  if-then tool for, 147–149
  new choices for, 145–146
  regulate step, 138–145

virtuous cycles (*continued*)
  spectator-awareness step, 131–138
  steps for, 130–149, 155
visibility, 38, 101, 125
vision, 1, 183–184, 204–206, 212,
  215
Vista Equity Partners, 4
voice track, 136–137
volatility, uncertainty, complexity, and
  ambiguity (VUCA), 7
Vynamic, 200

walking meditation, 142–144
Weil, Andrew, 141
Weiner, Jeff, 11–12, 96–97

white space, 142, 163, 197, 209
  in time and energy management,
    76–78, 83
  during travel, 89
Who Owns What, 98–101
"Wild Geese" (Oliver), 181
Wilkins, Muriel Maignan, 11
Williams, Serena, 61–62, 165
Winfrey, Oprah, 12
work products, 56, 58, 171
write experiences, 132–133, 173
Wu-wei, 10, 184

Yee, Rodney, 85
Your Brain at Work (Rock), 134

ACKNOWLEDGMENTS

The adage "it takes a village" could not be truer as I consider all the people who have generously shared their expertise, experience, and support along the way.

To the book development team, I am grateful for all that you have brought of yourselves and for the incredible team experience this has been. Amy Gallo, you have worn every hat possible throughout this process—coach, advisor, editor, and friend. You read countless outlines and helped me to transform it all into a coherent structure and flow. Catherine Knepper, you are one of the most gifted writers I have ever met. Somehow, you took every draft and transformed the ideas into lyrical and beautiful writing. Thank you for helping to bring my voice to life and make it sing.

To my brilliant executive editor, Jeff Kehoe, and the HBR Press team, I am so appreciative of the opportunity to work with you on a second book. You have helped me to shape the book's vision and provided critical counsel and perspective every step of the way. Thank you to Giles Anderson, my literary agent, who reached out at the perfect time and provided the catalyst to form a vision for this book, and the proposal to make it a reality. Your advice throughout has been appreciated. And to Jenna McMullan-Freedman, you have brought invaluable marketing counsel and support to me all along the way.

There are days I can't believe I get to partner with the leaders and organizations I work with each day as an executive coach. I have been humbled by the folks out there working hard, wanting to make a difference, and willing to explore who their best self is in service of growing and transforming their teams and organizations. I thank you all for the learning and growth I've experienced in knowing you.

None of this work would be possible without the sponsorship of executives who care about the growth of others and invest in talent. A shout-out to a few critical people. To Betty Hung, operating principal at Vista Equity Partners—a big thank-you for the last five years of partnering together to support your annual executive retreat. The spirit from those discussions is captured in these pages, and much of the wisdom here stems from your thinking on what leaders need in order to be the best they can be. To Jane Brock-Wilson and Sam Adams of Berkshire Partners—I am grateful for your sponsorship and mentorship through the years. You introduced me to the concept of a "highest and best" self, and you and your colleagues have shown me what it means to embody that.

I am also grateful to David Bradley, chairman of Atlantic Media, Nancy Disman, CFO of West Corporation, and Leeann Wurster-Naefe and Bill Pullen of the Georgetown University Certificate in Leadership Coaching program, all who afforded opportunities to engage with their teams to discuss key concepts in this book in sneak-preview form. From each of these events, I learned new distinctions, ideas, and ways that leaders out on the front lines are thinking about how to sustain and scale a best self.

There were many folks who helped to shape the content at various stages. To my dear friend Pat Gartman, thank you for the time spent helping to prepare for events so that I could bring this work to leaders in discussion form. To my cousin, Emily Lin, CAO of Citi-Lean & Smart Automation at Citigroup and an executive coach, you were the perfect person with whom to share and test ideas. To Carole Tilmont, who not only sponsors our work at Emergent Bio-Solutions but always asked for an update on the book, and sent me the perfect handwritten note at a time I most needed it. To Pam Krulitz, thank you for being a cheerleader and friend throughout.

To Emily Holland Hull, head of talent development for digital at Capital One, and Christine Britton, talent business partner at Optum, my thanks for taking the time to read the full manuscript from beginning to end and providing the HBR Press team invaluable feedback. To Rachel Arnold, principal at Vista Equity Partners; Dana Rousmaniere, managing editor, HBR Insight Centers; and Ann Bundy of the Paravis Partners team, I appreciate the early reads you did to help understand what would be most impactful.

To the Paravis team I work with each day, a big thank you. To Muriel Wilkins, my cofounder of the firm and coauthor of the HBR Press book *Own the Room: Discover Your Signature Voice to Master Your Leadership Presence*—thank you for the encouragement to write this and to bring my full voice to it. To Nina Bowman, fellow managing partner, and to our full team of colleagues, I am so lucky to be in the company of folks who want to make a difference every day. To Jenny Sheehan, EA extraordinaire, thank you for keeping me sane and working your magic with the calendar.

There have been many teachers who have helped me to more fully discover the leader I want to be. To Glenn Hartelius, founder of Attention Dynamics, you've been a critical spiritual guide. Thank you for the support through many chapters of life. Barbara Braham, your work in adult development theory came at the perfect time. To Brian Emerson, your friendship and work on polarities has enriched my thinking and development. Thank you to James Flaherty and Sarita Chawla, my teachers at New Ventures West, where I trained for my coaching certification and was set on this path. To Barbara Stanny, the life vision you helped me to craft back in 2010 is fully in motion. Finally, to my professor Mark Lepper, PhD, chairman of the psychology department at Stanford University, who first helped me to discover my love of human psychology.

To my parents, Neil and Lilly Jen, I couldn't ask for more supportive and dedicated parents. I appreciate your encouragement to dream and dream big. Your sacrifices throughout my life have opened doors for which I am grateful. And finally, to my husband, Greg Su, and son, Jordan Su, you are the biggest part of my living a full, rich, and meaningful life. I couldn't do any of this without your love and cheering me on every step of the way.

ABOUT THE AUTHOR

For almost two decades, **Amy Jen Su** has worked with CEOs, senior executives, and rising stars in organizations to sustain and scale their "highest and best" selves as they lead organizational change, growth, and transformation. A keynote speaker and seasoned coach for industries such as biotechnology, private equity, software, technology, and media, Amy understands the excitement and challenges of fast-paced businesses out to make a difference in the world. Amy is a managing partner and cofounder of Paravis Partners, a boutique executive coaching and leadership development firm that has coached and trained thousands of leaders across a variety of industries.

Amy is also the coauthor of the Harvard Business Review Press book *Own the Room: Discover Your Signature Voice to Master Your Leadership Presence* and is a regular contributor to the *Harvard Business Review* online. She has also been a contributing author to the HBR Emotional Intelligence books—*Leadership Presence*, *Focus*, *Confidence*, and *Mindful Listening*—as well as the *HBR Guide to Coaching Employees* and the *HBR Guide to Thinking Strategically*. She has also been interviewed by media outlets including the *Wall Street Journal*, *Fast Company*, *Spirit Magazine*, and *NewswireFM*.

Prior to cofounding Paravis Partners, Amy's previous business experience includes serving as a management consultant for Booz Allen & Hamilton, where she advised senior executives of consumer products companies on marketing and growth strategies. She was also a strategic planner for the Taco Bell Corp. and was instrumental in helping to launch Taco Bell into nontraditional points of distribution.

Amy holds an MBA from Harvard Business School and a BA in psychology from Stanford University, graduating from both with honors and distinctions. Her additional certifications in Integral Coaching, yoga, and meditation and her passion for the Eastern philosophies provide for a unique high-impact, whole-person approach to executive development.